A SHORT HISTORY OF MODERN ANGOLA

DAVID BIRMINGHAM

A Short History of Modern Angola

HURST & COMPANY, LONDON

First published in the United Kingdom in 2015 by
C. Hurst & Co. (Publishers) Ltd.,
41 Great Russell Street, London, WC1B 3PL
© David Birmingham, 2015
All rights reserved.
Printed in India

A Cataloguing-in-Publication data record for this book
is available from the British Library.

ISBNs: 9781849045148 *hardback*
      9781849045193 *paperback*

This book is printed using paper from registered sustainable
and managed sources.

www.hurstpublishers.com

CONTENTS

PREFACE

The history of Angola falls into three parts. In medieval times the region was ruled by kings who controlled the religious art of rain-making and the magic art of iron-smelting. The three 'early modern' centuries were dominated by Brazilian *conquistadores* for whom Angola was the 'Black Mother' which supplied millions of plantation slaves. The nineteenth and twentieth centuries saw the rise of a modern colony covering a land area of half a million square miles. Between 1820, when the modern era began, and 1975, when the formal colonial era ended, Angola's coast, and in time its whole territory, was administered by Portugal. This modern period is dominated by great flows of migrant peoples. In the nineteenth century over half a million Africans were taken from their homes as slaves, or as conscript labourers, to work the coffee estates of the newly independent empire of Brazil or the cocoa plantations of the little island-colony of São Tomé. The beautiful harbour-city of Luanda became the capital of a spreading Angolan colony ruled by governors appointed by the Saxe-Coburg kings and queens of Portugal. In the twentieth century the flow of peoples was reversed and up to half a million European migrants arrived in Angola. Many came from the back lands of northern Portugal, or the Atlantic islands of Madeira and the Azores, seeking prosperity in Africa. Others were later conscripted as foot-soldiers to resist the rising tide of anti-colonial nationalism which swept through Africa in the 1960s. Colonial governors from Portugal's army and navy were appointed by republican dictators who ruled in Lisbon after the monarchy had been overthrown in 1910. In 1975 change occurred again and the white population of Angola flowed back to Europe leaving African nationalists to struggle for control of their rich but unequally shared economic heritage.

The kingdom from which Angola gained its name was initially ruled by the Ngola dynasty whose rocky fortress lay above the valley of the Kwanza River.

It was first described to the outside world by an early Jesuit mission established there in the 1560s. The wealth of the kingdom was epitomised by the coastal fisheries of Luanda Island which produced a regional shell currency. Spiralled shells were used in the Kongo kingdom for such social payments as bride wealth and for political taxes or judicial fines. The Ngola's northern neighbour was the ruler of this larger and more powerful kingdom lying south of the Congo River estuary. The medieval customs and traditions of Kongo were recorded by Christian missionaries and by Jewish traders. The king received feudal-type tribute from half-a-dozen provinces whose governors soon adopted European titles such as marquis or duke. To the south of the Ngola's domains lay the great Benguela highland, ruled by a dozen merchant kings, and a coastline of Atlantic fishing villages. Today these three regions, north, central and south, are part of the Republic of Angola.

The Atlantic shipping bridge which linked Angola to South America grew slowly when Portuguese colonies called 'captaincies' were established in Brazil in the 1530s and cane sugar became the world's most valuable traded commodity. Initially Atlantic merchants bought their supply of Brazilian plantation slaves from the kings of Kongo. These kings, one of whom sent his son to Rome to be trained as a bishop, received European craftsmen and priests to build and staff churches which enhanced the prestige of their capital city, San Salvador. They paid for expatriate missionaries by selling black labourers. As this trade in slaves grew, a Brazilian-type captaincy was created in the 1570s at Luanda in Angola. This African estate was granted to the Jewish grandson of the Portuguese explorer Bartholomew Dias. His role as supreme lord-proprietor of Angola was later replaced by military captains appointed by the Habsburgs who came to rule Portugal, as well as Spain, in the 1580s. These *conquistadores* overran the Kwanza River basin, levied tribute in male and female slaves from local headmen, and gained wealth by selling their captives not only to the infant plantations in Brazil but also to Spain's great American dominions.

The Atlantic trade was greatly enhanced by the Dutch development of modern capitalism and the invention of joint stock companies which gained a major stake in Portugal's East Indies and later also in Brazil. Dutch shipping carried a significant share of Atlantic produce to northern Europe. In the 1640s the Dutch 'empire', which gained fortresses in both West Africa and South Africa, temporarily held the great Angolan fortress at Luanda from which it supplied slaves to rich sugar colonies which the Dutch had captured in northern Brazil. By the eighteenth century new discoveries of American mineral wealth required ever more slave miners. Brazilian wealth grew in leaps and bounds with the discovery of first gold and later of diamonds. Angola's slave catchers were driven to extend their commercial networks deeper into the interior of Africa. The old *conquistadores* were replaced as suppliers of slaves by Europeanised African merchants, sometimes referred to as 'Creoles'. In Angola black, Portuguese-speaking, Creoles were predominantly traders who imported manufactured goods, particularly cotton textiles from Portuguese India. A more corrosive form of payment for slaves was the addictive supply of tobacco and rum from Brazil and of rough red wine from Portugal. From the early nineteenth century the commercial sphere of informal influence dominated by Portugal, and by the Angolan Creoles, gradually evolved into a formal colonial territory, albeit one with fluctuating frontiers which were not finally agreed to by rival European powers until the 1920s.

The use of names in Angola presents a problem. Geographically the country's southern neighbour, Namibia, was for about a hundred years known as South-West Africa. On the eastern border, Zambia was once called Northern Rhodesia, and Katanga was briefly known as Shaba. The territory to the north of Angola went through even more changes of name—the Free State, the Belgian Congo, Congo-Kinshasa, Zaïre, most recently the DRC. In this book it is referred to throughout as Congo. This needs to be distinguished from a French colony variously known as Middle Congo, French Congo, and Congo-Brazzaville. Another possible cause of confusion concerns the name of different 'ethnic' groups. I refer to the Kikongo-speaking people of the north as Kongo and the Umbundu-speaking people of the south as Ovimbundu. I have, improperly, called the Kimbundu-speaking people of the centre 'Kimbundu' rather than using the more correct 'Mbundu'. Like every other historian of Angola I had great difficulty finding a term to use for Africans with a greater or lesser degree of Portuguese culture. I have controversially called them 'Creole' with apologies to all those who have tried to find alternatives. In the wider historical literature the term Creole has meant black in West Africa and white in the West Indies. It has sometimes been used to refer to the Luso-Africans of old colonial towns, to mixed-race Angolans with Portuguese genes as well as Portuguese culture, and even to the *assimilado* population which was legally assimilated into colonial citizenship. I have arbitrarily Anglicised the mixed-race term *mestiço* as *mestizo*, and not mulatto. Some Angolan towns changed their name for part of the colonial period but here modern names have been used—Ndala Tando, not Villa Salazar, and Huambo not Nova Lisboa or New Lisbon. São Salvador, or Mbanza

Kongo, has—quite illogically—somehow retained the sixteenth-century name, San Salvador.

The complex history of modern colonialism in Angola, and of the wars of liberation which followed, have been studied by an illustrious cohort of international scholars from a dozen countries. Pre-eminent among them was Jill Dias, a British historian married to one of Portugal's most distinguished scientists. She devoted a life-time to meticulous research and to wide-ranging teaching. Although she published thirty-odd learned articles, including a 250-page essay on nineteenth-century Angola, her aspiration to write a fully rounded history of modern Angola was cut short in 2008. She suffered a cerebral stroke while sitting at her keyboard and a whole generation of young scholars from Angola, and indeed spread across the globe, was left bereft of her wise counsel. It would be impossible to reconstruct the history which Jill might have written, and for which she had collected so many original documents and historic photographs. These are now preserved for posterity in the archives of the New University in Lisbon. As a tribute to her scholarship, however, this book tries to present a very short history of modern Angola. Two very eminent historians who do survive in Angola are Arlindo Barbeitos, who published a Portuguese collection of my old essays under the title *Portugal e Africa* and Maria da Conceição Neto who translated my thesis as *Alianças e Conflitos: Os Primordios da Ocupação Estrangeira em Angola 1483–1790*. It was São who read a full draft of the present book and made many improvements, for which I am extremely grateful.

My credentials for writing about modern Angola are varied and eccentric. The hundred-odd items in the bibliography were not electronically selected but are books which happened to be on my own shelves. One of the most imaginative of Angola's historians is the novelist Pepetela from whose works I have gained many insights. I have also visited all the provinces of Angola, even Cabinda, with the sole exception of Kwando-Kubango, the 'land at the end of the earth', to which some black intellectuals were banished in colonial times. One famous intellectual, who never was banished there, was the poet, doctor, and statesman Agostinho Neto for whom I acted as interpreter when he escaped from a Portuguese prison and arrived at the London office of Amnesty International as a 'prisoner of conscience'. While living in Dar-es-Salaam I coined the word Lusophone to describe Portuguese-speaking African nationalists. In 1963 my first travels around Angola were supervised by a tourist agent who worked for Portugal's fearsome political police. He allowed me to travel up to the diamond mines in the cockpit of an old Dakota and back again on the famous Ambaca railway. I also rode the brass-handled Benguela Railway to Bihé, re-named Silva Porto after a backwoods trader. Ten years later I visited the most famous of the Holy Ghost missionaries, Carlos Estermann, in his little house on the Huila plateau in the deep south. In Zürich I read the multi-lingual correspondence of Héli Chatelain, the nineteenth-century founder of the Swiss mission on the Benguela highland. I was able to explore the old coffee estates of the Amboim plateau where one of the most virulent of anti-colonial protests had taken place in 1917. I was, improbably, dining with international bankers in the Reform Club in London when, a few days before the Lisbon coup of 25 April 1974, I was quietly advised that Portugal's government was about to be toppled. I happen to have been in Luanda one April night in 1975 when a returning exile was 'welcomed' by hostile hot-heads who attempted to shoot down his plane but instead punctured holes in a South African passenger jet coming in to refuel. I later revisited the south in the austerity year of 1987 when Russian military advisers were propping up the bar of the Grand Hotel while South Africa's French fighter jets were circling overhead. A report I wrote at the time on the functioning of the informal economy was used as a planning paper by members of the Angolan cabinet. In the Luanda archives I studied the local records both of the northern coffee district of Cazengo and of the southern farming district of Caconda. My attempt to visit the Kongo city of San Salvador, and its eleven ruined churches, was abortive but I did take a boat ride along the Congo River from the oil-haven of Soyo. In 2003 I travelled to the Zambian border with two British members of parliament, stopping en route to see the place where the civil war had ended when Jonas Savimbi had been killed a year before. We later crossed the headstream of the Zambezi by canoe to visit a leper colony. Of such accidental adventures is the life of an historian composed. My travels were enthusiastically supported by my wife Elizabeth, and we lived for some months in Angola with our children. The text of this little book has been rigorously revised by my colleague Doreen Rosman. It is dedicated to the memory of Jill Dias.

David Birmingham, Canterbury, January 2015

TIMELINE

1483 Portuguese sailing caravels reach the west coast of Central Africa
1506 Afonso gains the throne of Kongo as a Christian king
1560 The first Jesuit mission established in Angola in the Luanda hinterland
1571 A donation charter for Angola assigned to Paulo, grandson of Bartholomew Dias
1617 Benguela established as the second colonial city on the Angola coast
1648 A Brazilian navy expels the Dutch from Luanda Bay
1665 Portuguese *conquistadores* defeat the king of Kongo
1770 Pombal, dictator of Portugal, confiscates the Jesuit plantations
1820 The Portuguese monarchy is restored in Lisbon after the Peninsular Wars
1822 Brazil proclaims its independence under Emperor Pedro I
1834 Portuguese revolutionaries limit the powers of the church and the crown
1842 An Anglo-Portuguese treaty outlaws inter-continental slave trading
1850 The Brazilian slave markets close under British pressure
1884 The Congress of Berlin restricts Portuguese influence in northern Angola
1890 A British 'ultimatum' bars Angola's road to the east
1902 The Bailundu War brings permanent colonial domination to the highland
1910 Portuguese republicans overthrow the monarchy
1912 The railway town of Huambo, later New Lisbon, founded on the highland
1917 North-eastern Angola granted to the Diamang diamond company
1926 Roman Catholic generals seize power in Lisbon

TIMELINE

1930   Salazar's dictatorship plans a new colonial charter
1961   Three rebellions break out in Angola
1974   Salazar's New State is overthrown by army captains in Lisbon
1975   Angola's independence is declared on 11 November
1977   Young radicals led by Nito Alves attempt a coup in Luanda
1987   One of the longest battles in Africa's history begins at Cuito Cuanavale
1992   A civil war truce allowed a general election to be held in Angola
2002   Jonas Savimbi killed and the civil wars end

GLOSSARY

Ambaquistas	Merchant families from the town of Ambaca near Luanda
Apartheid	Racial segregation
Assimilados	Africans who were legally absorbed into colonial culture
Carbonari	A working-class anarchist movement which felled the Portuguese Monarchy in 1910
Creoles	A controversial term which in Angola tended to refer to predominantly black Africans with Portuguese culture
Dash	a gift or bribe
Gastarbeiter	migrant labourers
Luso-Africans	people of mixed Portuguese and African race and/or culture
Mestizos	persons of mixed race (also *mestiços*)
Musseque	a Luanda slum
pidgin	a mixed language
Pombeiros	peripatetic commercial agents in the Angolan hinterland
Serviçal/Serviçais	an indentured conscript labourer or labourers

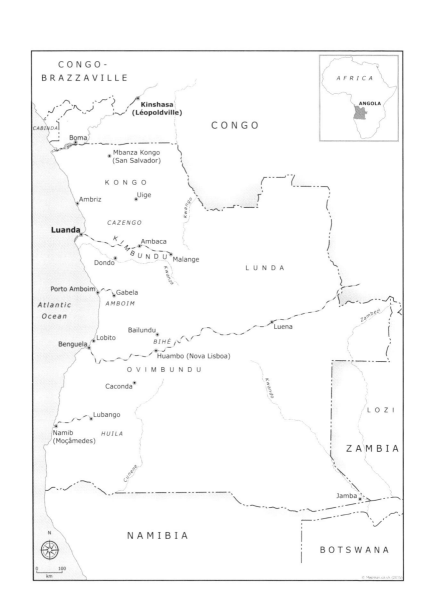

1

THE FORGING OF A COLONY

The modern history of Portuguese colonisation in Angola might be said to begin around 1820. In that year Portugal saw an end to the long aftermath of the Peninsular Wars. A Portuguese king, who had been in exile for thirteen years, returned to Lisbon thereby precipitating a constitutional struggle which resulted in the creation of a bourgeois monarchy whose members were related to Queen Victoria. At the same time there were repercussions for Angola from events in another distant land. In 1822 Angola's major trading partner, and Portugal's largest colony, Brazil, declared itself independent. By this time Portugal's old Asian empire, now reduced to toe-holds in China, Indonesia and India, was little more than a memory celebrated in epic poetry and haunting music. This Asian empire was very gradually replaced by a new African empire. The eastern shore of Africa had a surviving Portuguese presence, notably on the island of Mozambique and in the Zambezi delta. On the Atlantic shore, four centuries of trading in gold, textiles and slaves had left half a dozen islands, fortresses and harbours in Portuguese hands. Two harbours, Luanda in north-central Angola and Benguela in south-central Angola, each had colonial outposts in the hinterland that in time became the nuclei for a new imperial drive. As a Portuguese administrative presence spread slowly inland, about a quarter of a million Africans were classified as colonial 'subjects' who were deemed liable to pay tithes or poll taxes. All the while the white population of the emerging Angolan colonies remained small, probably fewer than two thousand Europeans. Nearly all of these were men, with very few women. Men were sent out as convicts, sentenced for serious criminal acts

1

or for engaging in subversive political agitation. Most served out their time as soldiers but some survivors stayed on in Africa as commercial agents and settled down to father large *mestizo* (mixed race) families. In Europe, meanwhile, poverty and civil disturbance fed a Portuguese impulse to emigrate but 90 per cent of migrants continued to move to South America rather than seek their fortune in Africa. Not until the second half of the twentieth century did large numbers of immigrants freely choose to settle in Angola. It thus took over a hundred years for Angola to become Portugal's most treasured overseas possession. By 1960, however, the colony's wealth matched that of the French empire in West Africa and the size of its settler population equalled that of the British in Rhodesia.

The slowly developing politics of the Portuguese presence in Angola often mimicked the African policies of Britain and France and by the twentieth century Portugal also adopted colonial practices from the empire of the Belgians in the Congo basin. One early theme of comparative imperial history concerned attitudes to the African trade in slaves. In the 1770s Britain decided that slavery could not be practised in the British Isles, only in its overseas colonies. The decision was partly driven by Lord Justice Mansfield who had black relatives by marriage. At about the same date Portugal made a similar decision. The semi-enlightened despot then ruling Portugal, the Marquis of Pombal, outlawed the holding of slaves in his European territories. He did so not out of humanitarian idealism but in order to retain valuable slaves on his tropical plantations rather than allowing them to be brought to Europe, for instance as exotic footmen in noble households. In France the law against the holding of slaves was more radical and for a while was even extended to the colonies. It arose with the revolutionary demands for fraternity and equality that erupted in the late 1780s. This French attitude, however, had extremely negative repercussions across the other European empires. Such was the panic that any tentative moves there may once have been to give civil rights to black slaves were eclipsed and the colonial nations came to dread every aspect of French radicalism. When in 1804 Haiti—the world's richest colony and the home of many slaves from Angola—gained its independence as a black sovereign nation, the imperial panic became endemic, especially in Portugal.

Colonial traders in northern Angola, and in the forest beyond, had greatly profited from being major suppliers of slaves to French Haiti. According to the popular imagination prevalent in Europe, northern Angola was the darkest part of the Dark Continent. Such was the growth of nineteenth-century geographical curiosity that no fewer than twenty-nine explorers from Germany alone set out to be, or so they claimed, the first white men to visit the unknown western spaces of Central Africa. The people whom they expected to meet were assumed to be barely human, living at an early stage of evolution from ape to man. The reality, however, was very different. Wherever they travelled the new breed of explorers found that traders had opened a plethora of trading paths dating back several centuries. They discovered that their guides could use Portuguese as a *lingua franca* to communicate with interpreters in most of the villages of the deep Angolan interior. Although many of the so-called 'white men' who had preceded them on the long-distance trade routes were actually of a blackish hue, they were considered 'white' because they wore shoes and trousers rather than travelling bare-foot and wearing loin cloths. Identity was effectively determined by culture rather than by pigmentation. The paths which these explorers followed were busy with porters carrying cargoes of ivory from the elephants they had hunted and of bees' wax robbed from hives in the high trees. The tracks were also used by coffles of slaves who had been bought in the interior in exchange for bales of calico.

After the hiatus caused by the French Revolution the move to outlaw the Trans-Atlantic trade in slaves began to roll again in Denmark around 1804. A similar law was soon passed in Britain, which hoped to stop all nations from trading in slaves. It feared that allowing colonial rivals to restock their slave pens would diminish any British advantage among the plantation economies. This economic motive was reinforced in Britain by an evangelical one driven by a movement of Protestant revival. In Portugal legislation relating to slavery went through the same stages of change as British legislation, albeit with years of delay. Whereas Britain outlawed the carrying of slaves in 1807 Portugal only began to do so in 1836. Until mid-century Brazil remained a major buyer of Angolan slaves and the numbers crossing the Atlantic actually increased in the 1820s and 1830s. In British colonies the owning of slaves was outlawed in 1834 but in Portugal similar legislation was not passed by parliament until 1875. In the British Empire life-long slaves were replaced by indentured workers whose term of servitude was theoretically fixed although the migrants, sometimes known as coolies, were not always given the opportunity to return home to the land of their birth. In the Portuguese empire indentured workers, known as *serviçais*, were often recruited for life. In practice modified forms of slavery remained ubiquitous in Angola throughout the nineteenth century.

In Portugal no enlightened evangelical lobby had pushed the anti-slavery agenda and although lay humanitarian sentiments were sometimes expressed little effective action took place. Portugal's liberals tended to vaunt their attach-

ment to human rights, and even to the rights of colonial subjects, but in practice their political leaders were dependent during the 1830s on the revenues
which could be extracted from the overseas territories. By ironic contrast it was
the conservatives of the 1840s who were willing to forgo colonial profits in
order to enhance their commercial relations with Britain. An anti-slave-trade
agreement was drawn up in 1842 between Lisbon and London according to
which the Royal Navy would be allowed to join the Portuguese navy in patrolling the coast of Angola to capture vessels which were still attempting to carry
slaves to the Americas. A mixed commission of lawyers was set up in Luanda to
prosecute slavers and thus it was that by 1850 Brazil had closed its ports and
the selling of Angolan slaves there had virtually ceased. Slave ownership, however, remained legal in the American cotton belt and on the Cuban tobacco
farms and so slaves were sometimes smuggled to northern America using ships
flying 'flags of convenience' which made them immune to British searches. In
Angola itself many people continued to be treated as slaves. Newly designated
'apprentices' were often expected to work for their former owners. Some of
these 'freedmen' continued to be sold to French colonies in the Caribbean as a
relatively cheap alternative to indentured labourers imported from French
India. Porters, wives, and labourers in inland communities were often effectively domestic slaves. Men and women who might previously have been
shipped to Brazil were taken instead to the cocoa plantations on the island of
São Tomé, five hundred miles north of Angola. Once there, their legalistic
labour contracts were regularly renewed by administrative fiat rather than by
any form of consent. Little real change took place in Angola until after 1910
when the Portuguese monarchy was toppled by a republican regime. By then
Portuguese colonial policy lagged years behind the policies of northern Europe.

Labour remained the central theme of Angola's modern history from the
nineteenth century into the twentieth century. Fear and pain were the incentives which drove Africans, who were no longer technically slaves, to work as
conscripts for colonial masters. Any economic incentives were limited and
unpredictable. Even when remuneration was promised it was sometimes in the
form of tokens that could only be used in a plantation store where prices were
higher than on the open market. When Angolan planters paid cash, sometimes as little as a few shillings a month rather than the few shillings a day
which became the norm in British Africa, the money was regularly clawed
back as a hut tax. Living conditions on the inland plantations, and also along
the coastal fishing beaches, were cramped and unhygienic. Nutrition was
monotonous and inadequate. Only the wealthiest estates, such as the big

cocoa plantations, provided even minimal health facilities. The laws governing slavery and conscription may have changed over the decades from 1820 to 1960 but the reality of an African life dominated by the prospect of punishment amounting to torture did not alter. The blood-curdling cries of white settlers calling for 'cheeky' workers to be soundly whipped, '*chicote, bom chicote*', rang down through the years. Victims, tied to the whipping post, were beaten with thongs of hippopotamus hide which each district commissioner kept ready for use in his office drawer. After a hundred lashes even the strongest man was liable to die of the wounds administered while the cowed plantation population looked on in dread. The life of an Angolan caught up in the colonial labour web was usually painful and sometimes short. One Portuguese journalist described the system in the 1920s as the 'economy of terror'.

The mid-nineteenth-century end of the trans-Atlantic selling of black slaves so curbed the value of African empires that some European powers began to contemplate withdrawing from their spheres of commercial influence along the Atlantic seaboard. Once more it was Denmark which led the way when in 1850 it gave up its great trading fortress on the Gold Coast. Britain had been tempted to do the same but a committee of merchants decided to maintain a presence in a comparable fortress. It was the Dutch who managed to pull out from the Gold Coast where they surrendered the oldest and most prestigious of all the great castles, the once-Portuguese citadel of Elmina. Portugal's greatest Angolan fortress, overlooking Luanda Bay, had formerly been held by the Dutch but it had been heroically recaptured by a Brazilian navy in 1648. The Portuguese were reluctant to surrender Luanda once more, or to lose international status by retiring from Africa. Their commercial activity temporarily subsided but a toe-hold was held and in the 1870s Portugal, like Britain and France, began to explore new colonial opportunities. The belief that there could be hidden wealth, especially African minerals which imperial rivals might aspire to extract, culminated in the 'scramble' for Africa of the 1880s.

Imperial governments, in Portugal as elsewhere, were always anxious to minimise colonial expenditure. As a result the risk investment devoted to empire in Africa was often handed to private companies, or undertaken by individual initiatives. The great magisterial companies in Portuguese Mozambique, in French Congo, in British Rhodesia, and in King Leopold's 'Belgian' Congo, were given almost unlimited sovereign rights. These rights permitted investors to compel African labourers to work for foreign interests to the detriment of their own freedom and well-being. Private-enterprise colonisation of this type was initially very limited in Angola. Benguela was governed by a provincial governor, and Luanda by a governor-general, both of whom ruled on behalf of an imperial ministry in Lisbon responsible for the navy, the colonies and the overseas territories. In the south-west corner of Angola only one company, using French capital, attempted to create a private-enterprise colony around the mid-nineteenth-century Portuguese harbour of Namib, then called Moçâmedes. The region, however, was a poor one and the experiment did not last long. Instead small autonomous communities of immigrants tried to make a living. Some were refugees who fancied that their economic opportunities might be better in colonial Angola than in the rebellious Brazilian state of Pernambuco. Others were Portuguese fishermen from the Algarve who thought that they could gain wealth by exploiting the cold ocean currents coming up from the south Atlantic. Yet another small-scale initiative brought island farmers from Madeira who hoped to make a living by colonising the little upland plateaux of south-western Angola. The most successful of the independent immigrants in the south-west, however, were neither Portuguese nor Brazilian but rather Dutch-speaking settlers escaping British rule in South Africa in the 1880s. These farmers, colloquially known as Boers, had crossed the Namibian 'thirstlands' in their great ox-carts and were to play an important role in Angola for the next fifty years. In the meantime, however, no further colonial endeavours by private companies were immediately attempted and when they were, in the 1920s, the focus had shifted from the south-west to the far north-east where alluvial diamonds were found.

The diamond fields discovered on the fringe of the Belgian Congo became a major source of revenue for the Portuguese empire. Diamonds had provided Portugal with great wealth back in the 1730s when gems were discovered in Brazil. Many thousands of imported Angolan slaves spent their lives up to their waists in cold water washing river mud for precious stones. It was Belgian capital and South African technology which opened the Angolan mines two centuries later. The colonial government gave a company, Diamang, virtually all the rights of a state within the state. Although the company's licence was not quite as comprehensive as that of any Mozambique private-enterprise colony, it was nonetheless extensive. The permission to recruit labour within a concession of several thousand square miles was absolute. To prevent diamond diggers from escaping home to their families and farms, or from smuggling gems out of the compounds, some workers were enclosed in wired prisons. The management of the enterprise was in the hands of white technicians, some of them would-be democrats sent into remote exile for political disloyalty to an autocratic imperial regime. In compensation for the hardship posting, these expatriates enjoyed a privileged life-style of segregation similar to that practised in South Africa. The Angolan mines were not quarried underground but were surface ones where the overburden of sterile soil was removed by huge gangs of labourers with shovels. The company was given a monopoly over diamond prospecting in the whole of Angola. The colonial government ensured that good quality gems would fetch the best price on the cutting and polishing market of Antwerp, and in the retail outlets of London's Hatton Garden, by giving a monopoly of selling to the De Beers consortium.

While company colonisation thrived in north-eastern Angola the small independent settlements of south-west Angola failed to prosper. The high plateaux were less disease-ridden than most of Angola but they were too remote and inaccessible for crops to be marketed. Subsistence farming rather than cotton planting occupied many white peasant immigrants. Their inland settlements also faced fierce hostility from neighbours. The Kwanyama, of the Namibian borderlands, were a constant source of panic until the region—in the imperial jargon of the time—had been violently 'pacified'. The coastland of southern Angola was initially rather more successful than the upland as a zone of settler colonisation. It suffered less from indigenous hostility and rather more from a dearth of local people who could be co-opted as workers. The fishing community came to depend on slave-type captives brought down from the Benguela highland to man the boats, mend the nets and cure the sun-dried fish. Conditions for workers were dire, drinking water sometimes had to be brought in by boat, the desert climate fluctuated from very hot to very cold, and ill-clad indentured labourers, living in straw hovels, frequently died of lung disease. The chances of escape were almost as limited as were those of workers who had been taken away to the cocoa islands. In theory conscripts expected to be allowed to return to their highland homes after two years of service, but they could never know when they would be arbitrarily rounded up for yet another lethal spell of service in the desert.

When the European powers began creating modern colonies in Africa it was Leopold of Congo who claimed that the art of colonising was to replace old columns of bearers with modern methods of transport, namely railways. His agents linked several navigable sections of the great river with segments of railway. In East Africa railway-building had been rather successful. The 'Lunatic Express' linked Mombasa to the headwaters of the Nile, via Nairobi, and eventually made Uganda a wealthy British 'protectorate'. The Beira railway opened up the Rhodesian chartered company estates to which Cecil Rhodes had given his name. The Maputo railway replaced Boer ox wagons in supplying coal and dynamite to the Johannesburg gold mines. In contrast to these eastern railways the three railways which were built in Angola had less success. The desert one climbed the great African escarpment to serve the tiny white inland settlements. The abortive dream of the investors, who included Cecil Rhodes, was to find Angolan gold mines deep inland which might match those of the great Witwatersrand reef in the Transvaal. This line was later extended by German iron masters but the iron mines they might have hoped to exploit never materialised. The highland railway out of Benguela took decades to build but eventually did reach the Belgian copper mines beyond the Portuguese frontier. In due course this British-financed railway even ran timetabled passenger services, with ornate brass-handled coaches linked to Central and Southern African lines running all the way to Cape Town. The most notorious of the three Angolan lines, however, was the Luanda railway to Ambaca. It was so extravagant in terms of metropolitan subsidies that Angola was mockingly referred to in Portugal as the 'property' of the Royal Trans-Africa Railway Company. For all its pretensions the company never did cross Africa. Since Portugal had neither capital nor heavy industry, the railway had to be built with British enterprise, British investment and British material. This could only be achieved if the Portuguese regime guaranteed a minimum financial return. With profits assured by the state, there was little incentive for the company to operate an effective service or even to supply adequate rolling stock. Worse still, the route ran over such unstable ground that land-slides or bridge failures often disrupted the erratic schedules. One hostile Portuguese politician described the track as a wide-open footpath used by smiling African porters trotting down to the port of Luanda with their head-loads of peasant-grown coffee beans. The contribution of railways to Angola's economic growth was later supplemented by motor vehicles plying the long sandy trails.

Portugal emulated other colonial powers not only in its railway building but also by claiming that its colonies were not really colonies at all but rather overseas provinces of the mother country. Such assimilation and integration had been most marked in the French municipalities of Senegal which elected members to the Paris parliament. Angola was also deemed at various times to be an overseas province of Portugal and as such was permitted to elect one or more members to the Lisbon parliament. The voters included not merely the white expatriates of the cities but also the more numerous Creoles of mixed race, or mixed culture, in the ports and inland towns. Voting, however, was scarcely an open competition and the imperial government was apt to choose approved candidates some of whom had never set foot in Angola. Nineteenth-century democracy did nevertheless have a local dimension and members of the middle class, white, brown and black, competed for seats on the municipal councils of coastal cities and up-country towns. This French-style establishment of colonial municipalities contrasted with British-style indirect rule by indigenous chiefs. Portugal did seek to make some use of African systems of political authority, but not with quite the panache which Britain gave to sultans and paramount chiefs in 'protectorates' managed by its Foreign Office, rather than by its Colonial Office.

Like other colonies, Angola was profoundly affected by the presence of Western missionaries. The roots of world religion in Angola did not date back to the rise of Islam, as they did in both West and East Africa, but to the arrival of Christian friars in the sixteenth century. Black Friars, White Friars, Grey Friars, bare-foot friars, even the blue friars of St John, all brought baptism and the Eucharist to northern Angola. The Jesuits and the Franciscans later brought Christianity to the Luanda hinterland. The legacies, much adapted by local religious practices, survived for centuries but by the nineteenth century religious influence had begun to change. Portugal had traditionally been an arch-Catholic country but in the 1830s the Portuguese church was quite severely persecuted by radical revolutionaries. In 1834 the government of Portugal dissolved the old monasteries in much the way that Henry VIII had dissolved the monasteries of England three centuries earlier. Portuguese monastic lands were transferred to the new bourgeois barons of the revolutionary parliament. In Angola, however, there were only limited church spoils to be appropriated. The great religious entrepreneurs of the eighteenth century had been the Jesuits. They had owned extensive lands, slaves and business enterprises in both Angola and Brazil, but in the 1770s the great dictator, Pombal, had closed the Portuguese chapter of the Jesuit order and allocated its economic resources to his family and to his political supporters. One religious order which initially survived in eighteenth-century Angola was that of St Francis, the Capuchin mission which had done much to bring Christianity to rural communities since the seventeenth century. The Franciscans did not have extensive merchant networks, like the Jesuits, but to survive with minimal subsidies from overseas they had to make their missions economically sustainable. This meant managing vegetable plantations along the rivers, a task which required the employment of slaves. The order dealt with the moral dilemma involved by claiming that Capuchins, unlike Jesuits, did not trade in slaves but, if offered slaves as alms, accepted them and put them to gainful use in their market gardens. When, however, Portugal's religious revolution hit

Angola in 1834 the last Franciscans were driven out and their slaves were heartlessly sold to Brazilian dealers.

In the second half of the nineteenth century new mission influences came to Angola. French missionaries, belonging to the Catholic order of the Holy Ghost, served predominantly in the far south before spreading towards the highland. In the north British missionaries were despatched by a Baptist missionary society which established a politically and economically influential church in Kongo. In Luanda province it was Methodists, led by American bishops, who created the tradition of chapels and schools among Kimbundu speakers. This mission was influential in training a generation of politicians, many of whom later switched from Methodism to Marxism. In the hinterland of Benguela it was American and Swiss Congregationalists of a Presbyterian disposition who brought hospitals and literacy to the highland. Here too churches had a lasting legacy in the politics of nation-building. All three mission traditions, Baptist, Methodist and Congregationalist, were to play a role in creating overarching identities in three broad regions. By the mid-twentieth century each region had developed a distinctive strand of politics which opposed the authoritarian, and largely Catholic, regime constructed by Lisbon.

The forging of a large and complex colony of half-a-million square miles in Angola took a whole century from the 1820s to the 1920s. By the middle of the 1920s the frontiers of the colony were finally fixed. The northern frontier, with Leopold's Congo, had been established as early as the 1880s. The southern frontier, involving confrontations with Germany and South Africa was eventually agreed in 1926. The complexity of Angola continued to be reflected in the contrasts between its three most populous, western, zones. The city of Luanda, which is described in chapter two, was the urban focus for the whole of Angola but related especially to the Kimbundu lands along the Kwanza River of north-central Angola. The northern lowland of Kongo, and of the deep interior, examined in chapter three, had quite different experiences, influenced by a range of foreign traders, explorers and diplomats. The south-central highland, the subject of chapter four, was extensively traversed by traders of many nations before being occupied by Portuguese soldiers between 1890 and 1902 when the great 'rebellion' in the Bailundu kingdom was crushed. Any eastward expansion, which might have been incited by the 1880s 'scramble' for Africa, was abruptly halted when in 1890 Britain delivered an 'ultimatum' which banned Portugal from pursuing its wider ambitions in Central Africa. The eastern frontier, between Portugal and Britain, was settled in 1905 by the King of Italy who had been appointed to arbitrate between competing claims to the region of the upper Zambezi. Thereafter two successive authoritarian regimes came to power in Portugal, Masonic republicans in 1910, and Catholic militarists in 1926, both of which aspired to transform Angola into a colony of white settlement, the theme of chapter five. Radical change only began to take root after the Second World War when a patriotic style of monetarism, initially adopted by the dictatorship of António Salazar, was gradually replaced by a multinational capitalism. Chapter six explains how this new economic dynamic managed, for a decade, to counter the rise of a multiplicity of nationalistic movements. The last three chapters focus on the battle for control of Angola fought not only between power-seeking indigenous leaders but also between protagonists in the Cold War. The colonial era ended officially on 10 November 1975 when the last Portuguese pro-consul departed. The colonial legacy lasted for at least another thirty years.

2

THE URBAN CULTURE OF LUANDA CITY

Luanda, according to Mary Kingsley writing in 1899, was not just the finest city in West Africa but was the only city in West Africa. It had been founded in the 1570s on a pretty bay with a long protective sand bar and a palm fringe. The upper town housed the governor's palace and the bishop's cathedral while the lower town had the customs house and the street markets. But even Mary Kingsley recognised that it had been slow to meet the modern requirements of a city and lay on a water system with stand pipes in the streets for residents. Street lighting, with lamps burning groundnut oil, was only installed late in the nineteenth century and the locals complained, as they had always done, that goats and even pigs roamed through smelly lanes foraging for edible garbage. But despite the backwardness in municipal planning the city was a place where quality trade goods could be sold. Mary Kingsley recommended that merchants equip themselves with fine linen, with coloured yarn, with velvet, with silver lace, with Turkish carpets, with coloured beads, with silk thread and with blue-dyed cotton cloth from the Guinea coast. She also advised her readers to stock up for a merchant venture to Angola on Canary wine, linseed oil, plenty of spices, and white sugar, not to mention fish-hooks and hawks' bells as well as pins and needles. Items made of English brass were much in demand in Luanda, as were those of pewter, together with every kind of haberdashery. The local toffs liked fine shirts, hats, and shoes for themselves, and surreptitiously bought muskets and gunpowder for their African clients. The question one must therefore ask is: who were the élite consumers of Luanda and how did a little harbour town of exiled convicts and wholesale slave merchants become the sophisticated city whose commercial opportunities were so admired by Mary Kingsley, the voice of British trade?

Three-quarters of a century earlier, Luanda's commerce had potentially been threatened when its traditional trading partner, Brazil, became independent. In the same year, 1822, the infantry and the cavalry in the Luanda garrison both mutinied and replaced the governor with an interim administration headed by the bishop. Portugal feared that Lord Cochrane, a British admiral then helping to free South American colonies from Spanish rule, might cross the Atlantic to seize Luanda. An army was therefore sent down from Lisbon to arrest the rebels. Once order had been restored Brazil reverted to selling Angola 2,000 barrels of rum and 14,000 cigars each year. Lopes de Lima, the author of an 1840s statistical survey of Angola, reported that textile imports had risen gradually to reach twice the value of rum imports, while wine and gunpowder each came to account for a significant share of Portuguese trade. Ninety per cent of Angola's exports were still made up of slaves, but Lopes also referred to foraged gum copal, bees' wax, ivory, and dye plants of lichen. Local traders still used raffia squares, spiralled shells and salt bars as currency but in the city copper *macuta* coins, worth fifty reis—one penny—also circulated. Each year the municipal market handled 4,000 sacks of beans, 4,000 of maize and 20,000 of cassava-meal. The population statistics given by Lopes are probably less reliable than the trade figures but he guessed that Angola had some 2,000 white people, of whom about 10 per cent were women, and 6,000 mixed-race *mestizos*, of whom half were women.

A more graphic account of Luanda in the 1840s was provided by another observer, a cultured physician with an insatiable curiosity. On 4 November 1841 George Tams, of Hamburg, sailed into Angola's magnificent palm-fringed bay. He was the ship's surgeon on a fleet of five merchant vessels, equipped with assorted trade goods, sent out to Africa to explore commercial alternatives to the trading in slaves. Financing the expedition had been difficult since the markets in London assumed that any vessels going to Angola would expect to trade in slaves though the traffic had theoretically become illegal in 1836. Many merchants at Luanda also assumed, quite wrongly, that they would be able to sell slaves to the German expedition. Tams, like Mary Kingsley, was struck by the colourful aspect of the city and its setting which reminded visitors of the great Bay of All Saints in Brazil. The town, he noted, was dominated by the fortress of Saint Michael as well as by the governor's palace with its adjacent cathedral. On the foreshore the imposing customs house opened off a broad terrace. The colony's only paved roads were two steep alley-ways lead-

ing from the harbour streets of the lower town, the *baixa*, to the official buildings of the upper town, the *cidade alta*. The dwellings of the merchants, all of
them still surreptitiously engaged in the sale of slaves, were brightly painted in
yellow and white with glazed tiles of red and blue which shone in the sunshine.
The tableau attracted the admiration of seafaring men who had spent monotonous months out of sight of land. Visitors also appreciated the fair-like markets
held on two wide streets. Housekeeping matrons, accompanied by their
domestic slaves, went shopping early in the morning when the fruit and vegetables grown on the Bengo river-side gardens were brought into town. One of
these great estates was the one that had been established two centuries earlier
by Capuchin missionaries. When, six years before Tams arrived, Portuguese
politicians expelled the last friar from the colony, the market gardens were
taken over by lay farmers who continued to supply the city with a cornucopia
of fruit and vegetables containing everything except the Irish potato. On street
corners around the vegetable market cauldrons of tomato soup were constantly
simmering and large market mammies sat under picturesque awnings display-
ing mats and baskets, knives and scissors, textiles and tobacco-pipes, and all
manner of useful household objects.

The city of Luanda, although a thriving market town, had no hotels or guest
houses and visiting dignitaries either had to sleep aboard ship or else find
lodgings with a hospitable householder. Tams was fortunate to be invited to
stay with Luanda's Spanish surgeon-general for the seven weeks of his sojourn.
This gave him unusual opportunities to experience daily life in a city dependent almost entirely on the labour of purchased black slaves and conscripted
white convicts. An educated middle-class German noticed many aspects of life
in Africa's premier tropical city which might not have been remarked upon
either by visitors from Portugal, the colonial overlords long familiar with
Angola, or by seamen anxious to get away from the heat and the mosquitoes
at the first opportunity. Tams was both fascinated and shocked by the daily
routine in a slave-run household. The day began at five in the morning while
the air was cool. The surgeon owned a horse and did his medical rounds for
three hours accompanied by a slave page who ran beside him. Horses were rare
in Luanda but one of the most influential of Portuguese slave dealers, a
Masonic political exile called Arsénio Pompílio, lent Tams both his horse and
his page to escort him to the farthest edge of the city on visits to the rather
grand *misericordia* hospital. The hospital wards were high and airy, private
rooms were available for those with money, and the wooden beds were fitted
with good straw mattresses. A little chapel had magnificent views out to sea

and across the countryside. Nearby a mean little hospital for soldiers contained fifteen beds which were usually filled with white convicts who had been given such 'satanic' punishment lashes that they commonly died. The military nurses were poorly trained and inadequately supervised by the visiting doctor. Although the hospital premises were better than those which Tams had previously visited in Benguela, where the cobweb-festooned pharmacy had little more to offer by way of medication than a few jars of Epsom Salts, the care of patients in Luanda did not greatly impress him and after a cursory inspection the Spanish surgeon-general and his German guest continued their journey among the fee-paying bourgeoisie of Luanda and arrived home for breakfast by eight o'clock.

Breakfast was presided over by Dona Catharina, the surgeon's Hispanic wife. The meal of veal and peppers was washed down with black tea and strong red wine from Lisbon. A small slave boy went constantly round the table filling up the wine goblets including that of the deep-drinking hostess. When all had eaten their fill, a slave-girl brought in a monkey who scampered round the table eating up the leftovers to the amusement of the guests. After breakfast Tams witnessed one of the most distressing aspects of daily life in a slave-owning household. Children who had, in whatever minor way, offended against the proper performance of their duties were taken down to the court-yard to be punished. Dona Catarina sat on her upper story veranda and relished watching her slaves writhing under the lashes of a whipping. The lady normally surrounded herself with small black girls, *negrinhas*, who engaged in embroidery. When one of them did not perform with the perfection madam expected she ordered that she be given a dozen beatings on the palms of her hands with the infamous *palmatória*, the wooden paddle with cone shaped holes which prevented an air cushion from protecting the flesh. On his first day Tams was so horrified by the screams of a tortured child that the punishment was discontinued. Dona Catharina protested, however, that a beating on the hands was 'mild' compared to other forms of punishment and that she only used the *palmatória* to discipline very young or newly-purchased children. The trainee seamstresses were expected to return to work immediately after their ordeal. When the Spanish madam had finished training and disciplining her child slaves she was able to sell them at a much higher price than did rival trainers. While Tams remained in residence, however, the beating of children was normally undertaken while he was out of the house. The perforated paddle, designed to instil terror into adults as well as children, continued to be used on both hands and feet for another hundred years

Household slaves worked long hours in the doctor's household but after breakfast the family retired during the heat of the day and snoozed until about four o'clock with a short break at noon for an English-style snack of beer and cheese. After sundown the main meal of the day saw the arrival of dinner guests who indulged in pretentious speeches and toasts. If the meal was appreciated by the guests the cook was called in and praised for his efforts but woe betide a cook who did not meet their expectations. After dinner servants who had been trained up to be sold, and whose physical condition had recovered after the harsh punishment regime, were brought to the dining room. The ill-educated guests discussed the merits of each slave paraded before them in the coarsest language and bargained with one another over appropriate bidding prices. Tams did not specify the nature of the 'coarse language' but some slave girls were purchased to gratify the lustful craving of their very male proprietors. When a slave was made pregnant by her owner she just might expect some preferential treatment but was not given civic freedom. Luanda households distinguished between *concubinas*, who were free women but not society wives, and *mucambas* who were slaves expected to submit to marital duties. Male slaves were also sold, and Tams described the men bidding around the dinner table as having hearts frozen by avarice which beat only for the sake of lucre. When their business was concluded the guests ate cashew nuts and mangoes, drank Angolan coffee, went for an evening stroll, and then settled down to play cards. At the card tables they drank lemonade, served until one in the morning by little slaves whose ages ranged from four to eight years old.

Apart from dinner parties and card games the slave-trading city had a rather limited range of entertainments. Tams referred to a billiard hall and a garrison gin tavern but made no mention of a bull-ring, though twenty years later the city did apparently boast of one. Many members of the merchant class were expatriate bachelors who frequented a dozen saloons run by Spanish or Portuguese madams. The girls had bright black eyes and sold wine and spirits as well as providing personal services. A few of these hostesses married their regular customers and thereafter, as they explained in coquettish fashion to Tams, ceased to provide sexual gratification since Luanda law allowed for the death penalty to be imposed in cases of adultery. In Luanda 'honest' women were carefully protected and the Luanda theatre had a separate entrance for married women with a barrier to shelter them from the gaze of male patrons. The city had once hosted a travelling company of actors from Madeira, but more usually plays were put on by theatre companies from Brazil. On Sunday evenings privileged members of society were invited to a ball in the governor's palace. Intrigue and jealousy were the order of the day among those excluded from the invitation lists while the black, white and *mestizo* guests became puffed up with pride. Tams witnessed one such ball and said that the military band played a 'horrible' fandango while the governor himself soon withdrew to his chambers, leaving his deputy to preside over the ceremony. Many of the ornately dressed crowd had begun life as vagrants, as slaves, as convicts or as exiled politicians, and most if not all had gained their wealth and status by selling slaves to Brazil. After the gala more lemonade was served and 'carriages' were called. The hammock-bearers, sleeping on the palace lawn, woke up at eleven at night to carry their owners home escorted by flaming torches. Tams commented unfavourably on the drawn-out farewells which involved ridiculous ceremonial formality. The governor's ball remained an important feature of Victorian Luanda for many years to come.

Several of the wholesale entrepreneurs in Luanda, as elsewhere in Africa such as Senegal and Mozambique, were wealthy women. Tams was particularly impressed by Dona Anna Oberthaly. She had been born in the deep interior of Angola but then kidnapped and brought to the coast to be sold into a Luanda household as a child slave. She told Tams that she had never been beaten in the manner practised by Dona Catharina, and that when she grew up, and contracted advantageous marriages to become a *grande dame*, she did not beat her slaves, a claim which Tams could verify by noting that her domestics did not have scars on their backs. Dona Anna's wealth, and the great pomp of her household, was financed by her success as a serious dealer in export slaves. An equally famous woman trader, though one whom Tams did not meet personally, was Dona Ana Joaquina da Silva, known as the 'Baroness of Luanda'. On one of her shopping trips to Rio de Janeiro Ana Joaquina allegedly spent the equivalent of twenty million Portuguese *reis*. Her trading activities not only stretched across the Atlantic but also deep into the interior to reach the empire of the Lunda people. She was reputed to own a thousand slaves and her assets were said, possibly with a degree of jealous hyperbole, to be worth ten times those of the colonial state. Ana Joaquina's palace and its grounds in the lower city were surrounded by a high wall to protect her property and symbolise her status. Her origins were apparently different from those of her rich and much-bejewelled colleagues, who had begun life as pretty young slave girls, since Dona Ana Joaquina may have had a white father. For a time she was married to a foreign resident in the city, but she built up her huge business enterprise as a very savvy widow who sent her children to be educated in Portugal. One of her trading partners was the Portuguese consul-general in Hamburg, the head of the firm which sent George Tams out to Angola to investigate alternatives to the newly outlawed trade in slaves. This expedition consisted of five ships one of which, the *Esperanza*, was later sold to one of Ana Joaquina's colleagues, the widow of a Sardinian medical officer who had been exiled to Angola. One of Ana Joaquina's own ships was called the *Maria Secunda* and may have been named patriotically after the then queen of Portugal, though the name was also one given to fashionable red-and-white Chinese necklace beads which she traded. Ana Joaquina's ship was undoubtedly used to carry slaves, and there are no less than ten listings of its appearances on the far Atlantic shore all the way from the Caribbean to the Rio de la Plata.

The Hamburg ships on which Tams travelled were registered in Denmark, once a major slave-trading nation, and carried the commodities usually in demand at African merchant courts as well as those that might appeal to city households. Among the trade goods which Tams listed were bayonets and sabres, shirts and skirts, felt hats and blue cottons, cigarettes and mouth organs, not to mention Chinese porcelain and beads. The cottons were often of poor quality and heavily starched. The ending of an old royal monopoly on ivory in 1834 had opened up a free market for one of Angola's most valuable products and Tams witnessed caravans carrying elephant tusks, attached to long bamboo poles. Ivory was henceforth one of a number of alternative exports to slaves. The Hamburg expedition may have been designed to explore such alternatives but everyone realised that the production and transportation of such 'legitimate' produce as palm oil, groundnuts, resin, timber, and coffee, were tasks still performed by slaves. Critics in the London press assumed that the expedition's trade goods from northern Europe would be off-loaded on the little island of Príncipe before being surreptitiously smuggled to the mainland to meet the demands of slavers still shuttling between Angola and Brazil. British merchants complained bitterly that slave labour was cheaper than the free labour now used in the West Indies and so claimed that their West Indian plantations would be ruined unless both Brazil and Cuba were prevented from replenishing their labour stock with fresh slaves. Dona Ana Joaquina had close dealings not only with Cuba and Brazil but also with Uruguay to which she sent a ship when she wanted to buy horses. These horses became important in Angola when her agents needed to travel quickly, and by night, to the small harbours at which slaves were loaded out of sight of British cruisers attempting, with the reluctant connivance of Portugal, to suppress the export trade in slaves. Permission to search United States vessels was not granted to

Britain until 1862, until which date 20,000 slaves a year continued to be shipped under the American flag to Cuba.

The great caravans which brought slaves from the remote inland marts fascinated Tams. He watched the columns arriving, each slave with his or her distinctive facial scar markings and speaking a distinctive language. Luanda residents recognised the remote ethnic origins of most slaves. Petty merchants coming into the city with just a few slaves sold some of them for rum which they consumed immediately 'like Russians'. Many traders were also addicted to the inhaling of tobacco snuff, and Tams noted that any cigar end which he discarded was eagerly seized and crushed to powder in a small mortar using an ivory pestle Although Tams does not mention it Luanda's Africans also chewed cola nuts as a stimulant. The large caravans brought as many as 2,000 slaves at a time and street scenes became very lively when huge crowds of guards and porters arrived back in town. The slaves were not always available for sale since many had already been bought by envoys, *caixeros*, who had been sent inland with large sums of credit to make advance purchases. Ana Joaquina appointed one of her ex-slaves as her agent to operate inland on her behalf. She also sent him several times to Brazil to oversee the final auctioning of her human property.

Tams wrote detailed accounts of the journeying of the slave coffles which travelled in single file along the narrow paths of the savanna. Their guards were festooned with bells to ward off carnivorous lions and leopards. Some of the slaves were required not only to walk to their own fated destiny on the Atlantic slave market but were also expected to carry produce for sale in Luanda. Tams could not always tell who was a slave and who was a hired porter though most slaves arrived in town with ropes, or occasionally chains, round their necks and with their hands tied behind their backs. Some slaves were linked together by long poles with forked ends that fitted around their necks. To minimise attempts at escape slaves were often required to sleep with their hands still tied uncomfortably behind them. The guards carried heavy guns and although these were mainly used to kill wild animals they did not hesitate to kill escaping slaves rather than risk being killed themselves. When Tams visited in 1841, the owning and trading of slaves was legal inside Angola and it remained legal for another thirty years. Since the export of slaves to foreign destinations had theoretically been outlawed in 1836, some caravan masters avoided attracting attention to the on-going export trade by bringing their slaves to the coast under cover of darkness rather than in broad daylight. Slaves who had been surreptitiously captured by neighbours while sleeping in village huts, and then sold to ambulating agents for a few bagatelles of trade goods, were hidden all over the city until it was safe to take them to a secluded beach where they could be loaded out of sight. Speed and secrecy were of the essence and most ships managed to sail away before rumour of the loading had reached the patrol boats. A report of 18 January 1845 claimed that a ship avoiding British detection arrived on the coast at 1.10 pm, loaded 450 slaves, and sailed again at 2.45 the same afternoon. One Italian owner was unlucky, however, and his vessel was sunk in the harbour shortly before Tams arrived. When a slave ship was wrecked the slaves shackled to the deck, as well as those in the hold, naturally drowned.

The governor-general of Angola may have had a low regard for the city slave merchants and only attended his own Sunday evening balls with reluctance. Entertaining a black merchant prince from the far interior was quite another matter and required lavish preparation and hospitality. Tams witnessed the arrival of one such embassy. The elderly prince rode in a gorgeous palenquin hammock with a much-tasselled parasol. His armed entourage consisted, Tams alleged, of 'one thousand' guards and escorts and the cortège was so impressive that the whole town turned out to line the route to the palace. The musicians led the parade with four-foot-long ivory horns, elaborately sculpted with animal figurines. Some of the drummers had double-ended drums which were held under the arm and squeezed to alter the tone. By contrast the 'great drum' was hollowed out of a huge log and the master-drummer sat astride it to play. The marimba thumb pianos had a range of two-and-a-half octaves, according to Tams. As the musical procession paraded through the streets it was showered with *macuta* copper coins from the upper windows and the prince's followers were able to quench their thirst with Brazilian rum. The people of Luanda sang and danced with youthful exuberance. The prince's portable throne was surrounded by four of the principality's government ministers. The prince himself wore a high royal bonnet to demonstrate his status but unfortunately one of his porters accidentally dislodged this 'crown' as he was alighting. The prince was met at the palace door by the governor-general with his attendants and an interpreter. A suite of rooms had been prepared inside the palace for a three day ambassadorial sojourn. The palace tables were richly laden with every kind of appropriate food. While the prince was entertained in style his entourage enjoyed the freedom to roam the town seeking urban amusements not available at an African court.

Not all Angolan princes received such an enthusiastic welcome from the palace. Tams was able one day to visit a little stone fortress on the foreshore which served both as a gun-powder store and as a prison. Seven of the prisoners were skeletal Portuguese mutineers undergoing dungeon incarceration while waiting for their death sentences to be confirmed by Lisbon. One prisoner, in a very dark solitary cell, was a royal prince who had fought a war with the colonial authority in Luanda over an alleged failure to pay taxes due to the Portuguese. He insisted, however, that he was not a feudal dependent of Maria II of Portugal but a loyal vassal of the king of Kongo and that he had therefore been wrongly accused of 'rebellion'. The governor-general did not accept this protest but once a month the prince was allowed to leave his cell and petition the palace for a reprieve. In his past life the prince had been an ally of the Portuguese and a 'general' in the black militia of auxiliaries who had done much of the fighting to claim territory for Portugal. He was entitled to wear all the braid and epaulettes of a Portuguese general. He wore this full-dress uniform on his visits to the palace and was always greeted by crowds as he marched forth in splendour. But his petition was always turned down, the governor having privately resolved that although he would not risk having such a distinguished prince executed for treason he nevertheless deemed him such a dangerous adversary that he would keep him in prison until he died of neglect, which he duly did some years later after a short reprieve. When Tams met the prince he was asked, in perfect Portuguese, whether fair hair indicated that Tams was an 'Englishman'. After the interview the prince was, as usual, returned to his cell where he had to surrender his uniform and once more don the rags of a convict. He may even have been attached to his cell wall with a chain.

In the course of his visit Tams would have seen people of varying skin colour on the streets of Luanda. The fact that colonisation had been almost exclusively male meant that Angola resembled Dutch-speaking South Africa in its legacy of racial mix. Many of the children of white fathers and black mothers learnt the Portuguese colonial language of their fathers, just as the so-called 'coloured' population of South Africa leant to speak Dutch. On a small scale Angola also resembled British India where white soldiers fathered Anglo-Indian children who over time left hundreds of thousands of descendants. In the British and Dutch cases, as well as in Angola, the consequences of miscegenation had lasting social and political repercussions. In the nineteenth century several thousand of these mixed-race *mestizos* were classified as 'civilised', an advantageous status which gave exemption from various forms of conscription, be it in porterage, street repairing or compulsory labour on the city vegetable gardens. Another high-status group in Luanda province were black people who wore shoes and were therefore deemed to be honorary whites—unlike those who walked bare-foot. The struggle to maintain status was partly economic but it also had much to do with a constant search for education. The city made little provision for education and the few private schools struggled when pupils tended to vanish rather than pay fees at the end of term. Literacy did survive, however, not only in the city but also in the provincial towns where people who regretted the passing of the great Catholic missions of old continued to teach their children how to read and write in Portuguese. Literacy gave the 'children of the province', the *filhos da terra*, some of them *mestizo* but most of them black, access to positions in the administration, in the military, and in the trading houses. A literate cobbler's son from up-country was even taken to America to help prepare a dictionary of the Kimbundu language for use in Protestant missions. He discovered however that his evangelical hosts, accustomed to the most rigid racial segregation, were utterly dismayed to see a black man arrive in their midst. In Luanda segregation was by class and culture rather than by race.

Some educated Africans in Luanda were members of the Creole 'aristocracy' consisting of the scions of families some of which dated back to the seventeenth century. They were readily employed as colonial administrators, officers and teachers and had the advantage that they were more immune to disease than any white Portuguese. The Creoles had the further advantage that they often spoke local dialects. In the nineteenth century some of the great families even owned private regiments of slave militias which could be used to further colonial aspirations at little cost to the empire. Creoles were appointed captains of the half-dozen forts which held the two-hundred-mile Portuguese enclave behind Luanda. They were also given directorships of the great 'factories' where goods were stored for the long-distance trade into the deep interior. These families greatly valued receiving colonial honours and titles in return for their services. Their main economic activity, however, remained trading, especially trading in slaves. Some owned provincial plantations that supplied the city with palm oil and black beans and grew the two American crops, cassava and maize, which were the mainstay of the urban diet and a means of feeding the human cargoes on the great slave ships. Some of the grand families had originally been founded by the Jewish merchants who came to Angola. One family which provided nineteenth-century Luanda with teachers and soldiers, as well as politicians and merchants, was the van Dunem clan. Their first ancestor had been a Portuguese refugee who had fled to Holland during a period of Jewish persecution and adopted a Dutch name. Around 1600 Balthasar van Dunem helped the Dutch to penetrate the

Atlantic trading system and chose to settle in Angola. Despite some notorious hiccups over the generations the family grew, became black, and prospered. In the 1980s one of its members became prime minister of the independent republic of Angola.

Another aspect of Angolan life which interested Tams was the legacy of Roman Catholicism. Three churches survived in Luanda though the richly decorated cathedral in the upper town, and the small candle-lit church on the market square, were not much frequented. The most prestigious Catholic church was the church of Nazaré on the northern fore-shore. The decorations were of vibrant blue tiles depicting the great battle of Ambuila in which the Portuguese colonial army of 1665, led by a Creole officer, had defeated the king of Kongo and his mercenary musketeers, who were also led by a Creole officer. It was in front of this church that the African élite liked to be seen on high days and holidays, wrapped in their finest cotton prints and wearing their most gaudy head-scarves. Services continued to be held under the authority of the 'Bishop of Kongo' whose seat had been moved from San Salvador to Luanda two centuries earlier. Two priests, one black and the other *mestizo*, were available to conduct services. Tams came to call on a day when the church was thronged with black African worshippers but the priests managed to squeeze him, as an honoured guest, into the corner of a pew and offered him Brazilian sweetmeats washed down with wine. This survival of religious practice was more marked in Luanda than in Angola's other coastal city, Benguela, where one of the two churches had recently been destroyed when the town had been severely plundered by a highland army. The other Benguela church, although ornately decorated, was little frequented and each *mestizo* priest who had been sent down from Luanda to serve the local Christians had died so quickly of local diseases that any attempt to appoint a parish priest for the south was abandoned.

Protestant activity in Luanda province began in the 1880s when a highly eccentric mission preacher, a self-appointed bishop called Taylor, tried to establish a self-reliant evangelical mission. As his city agent he appointed an escapee from the struggling watch-making region of western Switzerland. Héli Chatelain, who had worked in America as an interpreter among poor migrants in New York, offered his services to the 'bishop' as a polymath who spoke many European languages and understood Portuguese. In Luanda Chatelain soon became quite at home among working-class Africans and then went on to develop contacts with the middle-class population of the colonial city. He husbanded his meagre revenues, partially earned through selling watches, by accepting dinner invitations. The most rewarding of his connections was with the British trading firm of Newton and Carnegie. The English import-export house kept on good terms with the customs house, with the police service, with the city council, and with the Roman Catholic bishopric, by lavishly entertaining dinner guests. To enliven the evenings with intellectual conversations on science or philosophy the directors invited the impoverished Swiss missionary to be an after-dinner speaker and he thus got to know all the important office holders in the city. When he was taken ill, his contacts, right up to the level of the governor-general, afforded him a free bed in the great Luanda hospital. The Luanda carnival was celebrated on the eve of Lent and Chatelain watched wryly as his pompous white landlord was covered with boot polish and showered with corn flour by his wife's normally cowed friends. This carnival had been a prominent part of city life since the seventeenth century when licensed days of disorder allowed little black people to mock big white ones. The carnival remained an important feature of Luanda society a hundred years after Chatelain witnessed it but by then the white devils were no longer portrayed as Portuguese colonists but as invading South African soldiers.

For all Chatelain's skilled network-building the Taylor mission was not a success. When forty-odd evangelists arrived they were intellectually ill-prepared and materially ill-equipped. Their extreme beliefs meant that they were reluctant to accept modern medication so they and their children were soon decimated by malaria and dysentery. The American Methodist church eventually adopted the survivors and set up a disciplined network of schools and chapels stretching a couple of hundred miles into the interior. When Freemasons took over Portugal's republican government in 1910 they discovered that an official Methodist bishop, who had replaced Taylor, was one of their own kind, a member of a Masonic lodge as well as a preacher. The Methodist church grew from strength to strength and education enabled many of its members to seek work in the city and become a backbone of the colonial administration. In the meantime Chatelain obtained Swiss sponsorship to move his sphere of mission activity down to the southern highlands. Luanda's Creole élite meanwhile extended the city's commercial, diplomatic and religious influence deep into the interior of West-Central Africa.

3

TRADE AND POLITICS IN THE HINTERLAND

Seven years after George Tams, of Hamburg, reported on life in Luanda in 1841, another traveller, Ladislaus Magyar from Budapest, described the societies along the estuary of the Congo River. The trading communities he visited feared that he might be an English spy sent to report on the river harbours from which they were still shipping slaves, but in fact he was an ordinary merchant from Hungary. Magyar reported that the Congo trade was thriving in 1848 and he estimated that as many as 20,000 slaves a year might still have been leaving northern Angola. The traders, one of them an old friend whom Magyar had known in Uruguay, came from a dozen countries and had stocks of trade goods estimated to be worth two million Spanish dollars. Traders' lives, Magyar noted, tended to be short as they indulged in sexual and alcoholic excesses and were soon felled by the malarial miasmas of the swamps. In addition to selling slaves they maintained a brisk trade in palm oil which gradually became one of the 'legitimate' commodities which attracted modern traders to Angola in the second half of the nineteenth century. The metropolis of the river was at Boma, on the north bank, a Victorian city of some size and distinction. In the 1870s it became the headquarters of the immense trading association created by Leopold, King of the Belgians. Here Magyar witnessed columns of slaves chained together with iron neck-rings rather than with the wooden shackles used in southern Angola. Once a dealer had bought a column of a hundred or so slaves he washed them, fed them, dressed them, and forced them to dance to the music of drums until they were fit and presentable enough to be sold. The price of a strong male was an 'assortment' of goods,

27

known as the 'trade ounce' in West Africa, consisting of cotton, gun-powder, brandy, bone-handled knives, copper bangles and other items to the total value of about eighty Hungarian florins. Young women were enclosed in separate compounds, painted with red dye-wood, and taught the amatory arts until they could be locally sold for a suitable price to a polygamous ménage or to an expatriate harem. Female children were rarely sold abroad, according to Magyar, but were sent back to the slave-hunting grounds until they were of child-bearing age and could take part in the replenishing of human stock in the interior.

Dona Ana Joaquina of Luanda fame used some of her cohorts of slaves to create farms which grew crops to feed the city and the merchant vessels which called there. When David Livingstone met her in 1854 he was impressed by her apparent willingness to use her slaves productively inside Africa rather than sell them overseas in an export trade which he so abhorred. She bought extensive estates in Luanda province and treated the slaves who worked them so well that they enjoyed the prestige of being Dona Ana Joaquina's servants and did their utmost not to offend her. The *grande dame* of Luanda society did not, however, abandon her Atlantic interests and, unbeknown to Livingstone, her agents were still stationed up and down the coast where they became skilled at knowing how to dodge the naval patrols appointed to suppress the slave trade. Ana Joaquina's jealous rivals were sure that she was the richest landowner in all Angola and that her chain of trading 'factories' stretched as far as São Tomé. It was Ana Joaquina who put up the capital for an ambitious trade mission 700 miles into the deep interior of Angola. Her Portuguese associate, a Brazilian backwoodsman called Rodrigues Graça, reached the heart of the Lunda empire in 1846 and established diplomatic relations with King Naweji II. Old-style colonisers, however, were not thrilled by Ana Joaquina's various initiatives. Her sharpest critics were concerned that by growing sugar cane in Angola, and investing in the local production of rum, she was undercutting the profits which they made by importing Brazilian rum. Having risen to the top of the social tree, Ana Joaquina lived in her Luanda palace until around 1860 and then died on a voyage to Lisbon. Interminable law suits broke out over the multi-national web of credit and debit transactions which she had controlled.

The economic development of north-central Angola depended particularly on two provincial communities, one up in the foothills of Cazengo and the other down by the river at Dondo. Cazengo was important as the centre of a coffee industry, one which by the late nineteenth century was more successful than the other attempts to create an alternative to slaving, be it whaling, wheat growing, tobacco curing, rum distilling or even coal prospecting and copper mining. From a few paltry tons of coffee produced in the last years of Dona Ana Joaquina's life, the crop rose briefly to 11,000 tons in the mid-1890s. Initially coffee was a peasant crop grown under the high tree-cover of the Cazengo hills. Over the years, however, the white traders and black chiefs who organised the transport of coffee to Luanda, or to the harbours further north, established plantations. Farmers who imprudently took out loans to finance an increasingly prosperous life-style found that, when the crop failed, they lost their land to the merchants who had advanced credit to them. Coffee farmers became impoverished workers on what had previously been their own land. As the industry grew, the colonial government decided that the seventeen political chiefs of the Cazengo district were actually vassals of the Portuguese crown and that the governor-general was therefore entitled to make grants to white settlers of any land that appeared to be vacant. Controversial land purchases and land seizures proliferated, colonial influences grew, and by the end of the century it was said that no African chief any longer had any effective authority in Cazengo. When prices failed, however, the repercussions were felt in the city. The Portuguese colonial bank had a Luanda branch which invested heavily in coffee plantations since Angolan land was cheaper than coffee land in Brazil. Some speculators who took out mortgages with the bank were Brazilians who thought that slaves in Africa would be cheaper than the poor white immigrants from Europe who were now hired to help harvest coffee in Brazil. Thus it was that, twenty years after slavery had been nominally outlawed in Angola, one third of the Cazengo population, over 3,000 people, were still slaves. Ironically 300 of them were 'owned' by the English trading house of Newton and Carnegie, the firm which used to invite the Swiss Héli Chatelain to its dinner parties. Apart from the slaves the population of the district consisted of 100 Europeans, 1,000 free Africans listed on the voters' register, and something over 10,000 'other natives'. Modern communications reached Cazengo only slowly, first by a steam boat to Dondo harbour down on the Kwanza River, then by the jerry-built railway heading towards Ambaca, and finally by a telegraph cable up from Luanda. Colonial ministers in Lisbon had dreamt of a 'New Brazil' but this was not to be found in Cazengo: 3,000 slaves did not match up to 300,000 slaves still working in Brazil, and 3,000 tons of coffee did not match up to 300,000 tons produced by Brazil.

The second economic focus behind Luanda was Dondo on the Kwanza River. The southern margin of the river was used to establish moderately successful sugar plantations but the colonial authorities never managed to penetrate beyond the bank and into the land where local miners quarried valuable bars of rock salt. Dondo became the head of a caravan route leading south to the highland and to the trading kingdoms of Bailundu and Bihé. It was a collecting point for a range of foraged and hunted produce including ivory. Dondo was not, however, a particularly successful river port for the coffee growers since the trail from the north had to negotiate the expensive ferry crossing over the Lukala River. This ferry was owned by a powerful chieftain, Kabuku Kambilo, who not only had African legitimacy but was also a colonel in the colonial militia. Kabuku's role in the colonising process was interestingly ambiguous as the Luanda government fluctuated between thinking that the future lay in the hands of settlers and believing that the future lay in the hands of land-owning chiefs. When the colonial impulse revived in Angola in the 1880s the chiefs lost out. The colonisers even built a bridge across the Lukala River and deprived Kabuku of a significant revenue stream. As settlers moved in, restlessness broke out among dispossessed land-owners. Matters were made worse by a devastating epidemic of sleeping sickness along the river. The small steamer service, which had been established in 1867, proved so unreliable that the railway pioneers built a spur on their Ambaca line to reach Dondo. In theory the train carried passengers as well as goods but when Héli Chatelain tried to ride the line, after coming up river on the steam boat and enjoying a holiday on a lush sugar plantation, he missed the weekly connection. For some years, however, trade at Dondo remained brisk and the little town appeared wealthy. Many of the river-side traders belonged to Jewish families from Portugal or the Atlantic islands and many of the streets were given Jewish names.

While the Cazengo coffee and Dondo sugar industries enjoyed limited success, the attempt to revive copper mining in Kongo was a dismal failure. Copper had been mined there on a small scale in the seventeenth century and in the 1850s a British firm tried to exploit the mine again. The West African Malachite Copper Mining Company built an iron loading-pier on the coast at Ambriz and hired a thousand bearers to carry all the necessary parts of a steam engine and water pump into the interior. Each porter received ten handkerchiefs and 300 blue beads for each 130-miles round trip during which he was expected to carry half a hundredweight of equipment. The management would have liked to use donkeys, mules and even camels from the Cape Verde Islands but all died. When the miners set up camp they hired houseboys from Cabinda as servants and washermen. These Cabindans were paid in

Manchester cloth which they sold on in exchange for child slaves costing twenty-eight yards each. To operate the mine the company recruited ten Cornish miners but failed to equip them with mosquito nets as a result of which the men soon died of malaria. The mine manager, J.J.Monteiro, was much better supplied and he and his wife were carried up to the mine with all the necessary equipment for their comfort, nets, tents, portmanteaux, bedding, soap, an India rubber inflatable bathtub, and a set of cane chairs made in Madeira. The costs in money and men were enormous but whereas the old Kongo artisans had extracted a hundred or more tons of ore each year the company produced no copper and eventually went bankrupt.

The Ambaca district of Angola, nearly 200 miles inland from Luanda, was very different from other northern territories. Unlike many Angolans who lived under the authority of headmen, chiefs and princes, people in this area did not obey 'traditional' rulers nor did they worship 'traditional' gods. They considered themselves to be 'Portuguese', *moradores*, and to be the loyal subjects of the Portuguese king. Most of them were black and were sometimes spoken of disparagingly by proud, white, Portuguese. A significant minority of 'Ambaquistas' were mixed-race *mestizos* and were sometimes seen by explorers from northern Europe, including David Livingstone, as inferior to true black Africans. Although only a small proportion of the Ambaca citizens had a close white ancestor, most of them spoke Portuguese with greater or lesser fluency. In contrast to the Gold Coast, where Portuguese words were incorporated into a 'pidgin' language mixed with English, spoken Portuguese in Angola remained relatively stable. More strikingly many Ambaquistas wrote Portuguese as well as speaking it and some of their archives are still preserved in Lisbon. The German explorers who travelled the Ambaca trade paths noted that the caravan leaders all carried quills, ink and paper. When their supplies ran low they made their own ink from gun-powder and wrote on the dried leaves of palm trees. They acted as secretaries to indigenous princes, and even served the great ruler of the Lunda 'empire'. These Ambaquistas were not only important as scribes but also as interpreters. They all spoke the Kimbundu language of their maternal ancestors as well as the Portuguese *lingua franca* of traders, travellers and explorers. In addition to being literate the Ambaca people were very proud of being Christian. They may not have practised day-to-day Christian worship but being baptised was an important feature of their special identity. Monogamy was much less prized, however, and an Ambaca trader often had a wife and family in each of the great trading entrepôts that stretched throughout Angola. The most active of the traders aspired to travel across the country once every year or two, maintaining good relations with the ruler of each chiefdom. In addition to language and religion, the Ambaquistas carried with them European architectural traditions and built themselves square houses, with windows, in sharp contrast to the often large and magnificent round ones built by the 'aboriginal' Angolan élites.

One striking feature of Ambaca identity, particularly noted in sketches and early photographs, was their sartorial style. The symbolic importance of footwear persisted into the nineteenth century. Ambaca people always wore shoes and to keep up appearances the role of cobbler was important. Leather-tanning and shoe-making were skills introduced to the trade entrepôts of the interior so that any Ambaca trader could present himself at each political court properly shod. Ambaca travellers also needed to be proficient tailors. They wore neatly sewn shirts and immaculately cut coats, or even overcoats. Equally important was the need to wear sharp trousers on important public occasions rather than the everyday loin cloth of raffia. When bouts of racism later pitted illiterate immigrants against educated Africans, it was black youths wearing trousers who were most at risk of being attacked by gangs of white vigilantes. In addition to shoes and trousers, the citizens of Ambaca also wore broad-brimmed straw hats. This status symbol was quite different from the high-status hats worn by the chiefs with whom they did business. Another feature of wealth and prestige was the mode of travel adopted. Ordinary people, farmers, fish-wives, salt miners, and slaves all walked everywhere, slowly covering up to ten miles on a good day. Ambaquistas walked too, but if very rich they could travel in a palanquin hammock. The hammock was slung from a stout pole carried by relays of strong men, two of whom could carry a high-status Ambaquista, or a foreign explorer, over rough ground at speed. Hammock-bearers were sometimes accompanied by guards, armed with double-barrelled shot-guns made in Birmingham. Some hammocks had canopies and curtains to keep off the sun, or shield them from the staring eyes of village children. The use of hammocks was made necessary by the scarcity of transport animals. David Livingstone, who crossed Angola in 1854, objected, however, to being carried and instead rode awkwardly on a riding ox trained by the Ambaquistas. Livingstone's ox was called Sinbad and had a notoriously bad temper. Some Ambaquistas managed to hire donkeys and a few even imported horses but the climate did not suit them well. The difficulty of keeping pack animals was such that abortive attempts were occasionally made, as at the copper mine, to introduce camels into Angola.

The great caravans led by Ambaca merchants faced significant transport challenges when carrying alcohol and cotton into the interior. The return 'commodity' had consisted historically of slaves who were driven like cattle. As the trade in slaves was gradually replaced by a 'legitimate' trade in ivory, the heavy and expensive loads needed not only to be carried but also carefully protected by armed guards. Following the development of a free market in ivory in the 1830s it became profitable to fetch tusks from far deeper in the interior but this involved ever more negotiations over porterage. A second legitimate commodity which came to the fore when the Brazilian slave market closed down was bees' wax. It was not until the 1860s that Rockefeller invented paraffin oil for lamps. Before that Angola sold quantities of candle wax. The next commodity to be traded was rubber, initially the vine rubber of the forests and later the root rubber of the savannahs. Rubber and wax were heavy to carry, like ivory, but they earned lower profit margins with which to pay for porters. To assemble a team of long-distance porters it was sometimes possible to buy slaves from a dealer who no longer had an export market. Bought slaves could be cheaper than the annual fee for hired conscripts from the state carrier corps. Assembling a caravan of porters, sometimes a thousand strong, was a slow process and in the weeks it took to muster a team those who waited for the departure date had to be housed and fed. Even once the caravan was under way delays were common. Each river crossing, whether by bridge or canoe, was liable to incur tolls which had to be negotiated. In some places previous caravans had left legacies of mistrust by abusing villagers and peace had to be restored, sometimes at considerable cost and with several rounds of rum. In the villages fear of witchcraft and sorcery was ubiquitous and any caravan thought to be carrying evil spirits suffered harassment and legal expense. When porters protested at the excessive weight of each load, or at the distance they were expected to cover each day, too much coercion led to rebellion and too little to a further slowing of progress. Weather conditions could make or break a caravan's profit margin as happened in the great drought of 1860. Epidemics could be even more devastating than drought or flood, and nineteenth-century Angola saw occasional plagues of smallpox as well as sleeping sickness. Theft was ever a problem with a few gills of red wine being siphoned off a barrel or a few lengths of calico being cut off a bale. Attacks by bands of brigands, intent on seizing a whole caravan, were not unknown. Another great risk involved the need to assign partial loads of trade goods to agents known as *pombeiros*. They needed to be credit-worthy when exploring all the by-ways of the great merchant network that was Angola. Although ivory, wax and rubber became the major export items of Angola's international trade, internal trade retained many of its historic features. Salt was always a key commodity as shown in the oral traditions of the Lunda empire which dwell on the pioneers who discovered remote salt pans. Thirty-kilogram loads of salt could be used to measure the price a slave. Child slaves, who were easy to train, were valued and could be purchased at about two bars of rock salt per year of age. To buy a good tusk of ivory it might be necessary to sell up to half a dozen slaves.

One scion of the great Luso-African families of the Ambaca diaspora was Lourenzo Bezerra whose trading career spanned half a century. He was familiar with all the towns of the old hinterland of Luanda and at an early age established good relations with the principalities of the Lunda 'commonwealth' at the heart of Africa. The great Lunda 'emperor', Naweji II, who governed the deep interior from 1821 to 1852, asked Bezerra to supply his court not only with western cattle but also with good quality dogs and hens. In the 1840s it was Bezerra who enabled the first official Portuguese embassy, financed by Dona Ana Joaquina, to reach the Lunda court. Bezerra enhanced the royal gardens by establishing fields of pumpkins and tobacco. Equally significantly he also introduced education, including mathematics and craft apprenticeships, to the city. His clients learnt how to spin and weave cotton and how to tailor clothing. Carpentry was another western skill that Bezerra brought so that chairs and chests could be locally fashioned. Even more popular was his ability to teach rum distilling and cigar rolling. Such was his status that Bezerra married one of the Lunda royal daughters and built a village of his own with fifty compounds near the queen mother's royal estate. He added ivory to his original slave business and over his life-time apparently bought no fewer than 600 tusks, some from the famous Luba people of the upper Congo. When he could not recruit reliable carriers for long distance stretches he hid hoards of ivory in the beds of streams. When, on one occasion, he went to retrieve a hoard, the Lunda emperor provided him with a caravan of 2,000 porters and an armed escort led by no less than five noblemen. Other members of the Bezerra family became familiar with the great trade paths and so enabled a generation of European surveyors, prospectors, explorers, diplomats and fortune hunters to map out the land that was to become Portuguese Angola in the twentieth-century. The greatest of these travellers was a former head of the Luanda public works department, Dias de Carvalho, who spent four years exploring the Lunda empire in the 1880s. His eight stout, illustrated, volumes covered everything from language and climate to ethnography and economy. Scholarship, however, was by no means confined to white explorers and one well-furnished Ambaca household contained not only the epic poems of Camoes, and the scientific works of Humboldt, but also atlases, maps, and English dictionaries.

England had traditionally been Portugal's most valued ally, but the development of trade in Angola contributed to a series of political and diplomatic spats. From the 1840s the British government had sought to prevent slave-trading by patrolling the Angolan coastline. The northern harbour of Ambriz, ruled by a marquis only loosely allied to Portugal, was a major assembly point for slaves awaiting shipment to the Americas and the Lisbon government had reason to fear that the British might seize it. In 1855 Portugal opportunistically decided that while Britain was enmired in the Crimean War it would be a good moment to lay claim to Ambriz. The British Foreign Office retorted that Portugal had no 'effective' presence on which to base such a claim, to which the Portuguese Foreign Office replied that it was not aware that Britain had had any 'effective' occupation on the Falkland Islands, to which it had recently laid claim. Lord Palmerston, Britain's peppery prime minister, held fairly negative attitudes towards the Portuguese and was once reported to have said that he found it expedient occasionally to administer a sound chastisement to the semi-barbarous nations of the world. He was referring not only to China but also to Portugal. Lisbon suggested that the matter of the Kongo coast be submitted to neutral, international, arbitration but Britain flatly refused the suggestion for fear that the case should go against the British interest, as indeed did two later arbitration decisions concerning Guinea and Mozambique. Instead the two parties battled out a compromise in which Portugal took control of the port of Ambriz but guaranteed not to allow access to the great slaving ships. Twenty-odd years later this agreement on limiting the trade in slaves and slave-like labourers was still a dead letter as Henry Morton Stanley, the American explorer of the Congo, reported while visiting Angola in the 1870s. His blunt opinion was that while Portugal was— of course—passionately opposed to the horrendous trade in human flesh it had no means of impeding the daily business of smugglers. He also pointed out that Portuguese settlers in Angola used slaves extensively and would rise up in rebellion if the authorities tried to interfere with their business activities. At the time much 'human freight' was being shipped under the guise of 'indentured workers' to the cocoa islands but Stanley preferred to blame the sale of 'coolies' for São Tomé on 'Portuguese Africans' rather than on genuinely 'European' Portuguese. Stanley also trotted out an old mantra which claimed that by buying convicts from the African tribal law courts Portuguese traders were saving condemned men and woman, especially witches, from death by execution.

The diplomatic spat over the control of Ambriz was followed by a wholesale political crisis throughout the kingdom of Kongo. When Henry II of Kongo died in 1857 two of his nephews claimed the throne in the conventional matrilineal style which insisted that a king's successor should be the son of one of his sisters. One such nephew, Pedro, was a moderniser who had good relations with the Portuguese and wanted missionaries sent to the court to ensure a Christian coronation. He managed to obtain the royal paraphernalia, the crown and the throne. His rival, Alvaro, did not favour a Portuguese connection but had good links with French slave traders at Boma on the Congo River who were shipping 'free blacks' to the Caribbean planters of Martinique. The French provided Alvaro with enough good quality textiles to bribe the Kongo electors into choosing him, rather than Pedro, as their king. A third party in the negotiations, Prince Nicholas, was not himself a candidate since he was a son of Henry II, not a nephew. In 1845 Nicholas had been sent to Lisbon for his education and he now served as a senior civil servant in the Luanda administration. Although Nicholas supported the Portuguese candidate, Pedro, he protested that the Portuguese were quite wrong to think that Pedro was a vassal of the king of Portugal. The two kingdoms were equal allies, he said, and had been so since the sixteenth century. Kongo was not to be seen as subservient to Portugal in the feudal style. When Nicholas's protest at the Portuguese claim to sovereignty over Kongo was published in Lisbon, the news trickled down to Luanda and caused uproar. The Brazilian consul-general in the city warned the prince that white animosity might endanger his liberty and that he would be wise to escape from Luanda. Nicholas fled up the coast to take refuge in an American trading post and hoped that a Royal Navy patrol vessel might ferry him to safety. This was not to be, however, and a military unit loyal to Prince Alvaro threatened to burn down the foreign trading post unless the hapless American merchants handed over the refugee prince. Nicholas was summarily executed and Alvaro's men appeared to be in the ascendancy. The governor-general at Luanda took fright and immediately sent an armed expedition into Kongo to protect Prince Pedro, his preferred candidate for the throne. The expedition was initially too small to be effective and the governor-general decided to accompany reinforcements but they too were worsted and the governor-general himself was wounded in battle. This catastrophe was so damaging to the *amour propre* of Portugal that Lisbon felt obliged to send an expensive European expeditionary army out to Africa to ensure its diplomatic ascendancy at San Salvador, the Kongo capital, and to repel the encroachment of French commercial interests. The European regiment fought its way across

Kongo to deprive Alvaro of the capital city. This was already but a shadow of its former self and its population, once estimated at 18,000 souls, had dwindled. The eleven long-ruined churches dedicated to St Joseph, St John, St James, St Michael, the True Cross, the Immaculate Conception, the Rosary, the Holy Ghost, the Redemption and the Misericordia had never been rebuilt and even the great cathedral was semi-derelict. The Portuguese soldiers found that further damage had been inflicted on the decaying royal city by Alvaro's force, and in the fighting the centuries-old royal archive was apparently burnt down. Eventually Prince Pedro was crowned by two Catholic missionaries with the name Pedro V, and he reigned over his capital city, if not over his fragmented country, for the next thirty-odd years. Portugal decided that the cost of occupation was too great since half of its complement of 750 soldiers had died of disease within the year. When it withdrew a colonial fortress was retained in the south of the kingdom and named after Pedro V, but this was Pedro V of Portugal, not Pedro V of Kongo.

It had been unusual for a governor from Portuguese Luanda to lead an army to war in the interior as had happened in Kongo in 1860. The hundred-odd governors who ruled Angola after 1820 mostly lived comfortably in their palaces, served on average for two years, and had minimal impact on territorial expansion. They were, nonetheless, rewarded with a salary which amounted to one fifth of Angola's entire budget. This bounty was supposed to discourage them from illegally engaging in trade to the detriment of a merchant class which was operating ever further into the hinterland. The policy did not always have the intended effect and many governors continued to earn a significant bounty from illicit commercial activity. One controversial governor, however, not only desisted from trading in slaves himself but even tried to apply a law outlawing the export trade to others, thus causing such a furore that he had to sail hastily back to Lisbon. After the high human cost, not to mention the high financial cost, of attempting to impose domination over Kongo in the 1860s further adventurism was discouraged for a generation. The next governor-general who did make his mark was Ferreira do Amaral who governed sternly for four years from 1882 at the height of the scramble for Africa. He was a man of colonial experience who had once served as a junior commander in Angola's far south where he had attempted to encourage the immigrant communities, notably in the fishing industry. When he became governor-general he aspired to establish inland agricultural settlements for European convicts. He soon came to recognise, however, that future prosperity would lie not in the hands of convicts but rather in the hands of free migrants. He decreed that settlers who needed slave-like labourers should be granted indentured workers on five-year contracts which could be legitimately and automatically renewed wherever and whenever they were required. This policy of virtually permanent conscription caused such a virulent workers' rebellion on the south coast that he decided to react harshly. He ordered that no fewer than 400 'trouble-makers' should be shipped to Mozambique. For an Angolan this was the ultimate punishment, exile as a militia soldier required to fight in a distant colony.

In the 1880s, still within the life-time of Pedro V of Kongo, one episode in Portugal's renewed search for overlordship was a draft Anglo-Portuguese treaty drawn up in almost comical style by two members of European royal households, neither of whom had any experience in African affairs. The envoy in London of 'the most faithful king of Portugal and the Algarve' was described—to demonstrate the importance of the draft treaty—as a peer of the realm, an honorary secretary of state, a commander of the noble and illustrious order of St James, a representative of the grand cross of Charles III, and the holder of merit awards for science, literature and the arts. His opposite number, representing 'the queen of Britain and empress of India', was Lord Leveson, earl of Granville, a knight of the garter, Lord Warden of the Cinque Ports, constable of Dover Castle, chancellor of London University, and secretary of state for foreign affairs. These two dignitaries agreed that Portugal would allow all trade conducted by any nation to flow out of Kongo, both to the coast and down the Congo River, without let or hindrance of any kind other than the payment of the customs dues imposed by Portugal on its own citizens. Every assistance would be given by the Portuguese authorities to any vessel, whether sail or steam, that was wrecked on the coast or in the river and no duty would be charged on any goods salvaged.

The draft treaty was intended to facilitate the commodity trade of Holland, France and England which had grown in volume since the outlawing of slavery in North America in the 1860s. In exchange for Dutch gin, French wine or Manchester cotton, Holland, France and Britain bought thousands of tons of 'legitimate' produce. A leading Dutch firm had twenty-six trading posts along the river and down the coast. In one year a French firm bought 1,500 tons of shelled peanuts, fifty barrels of rubber and twenty-five tons of ivory. Hatton and Cookson of Liverpool were one of several English enterprises whose agents bought palm oil in particular. The traders of all nations, would be allowed, under the terms of the proposed Anglo-Portuguese treaty, to establish merchant factories, to travel unhindered, and to buy land on which to set up family households. Portugal would be permitted to raise any tolls required to manage river navigation but would not charge duty on any goods merely in transit through its territory. Equally important and controversial was a clause that insisted that missionaries of every Christian denomination should be allowed to evangelise freely in all territory granted to Portugal and be permitted to open consecrated burial grounds, chapels, and schools for converts. The revealing sting in the tale of the draft treaty was Article XII in which the Portuguese agreed to do all in their power to help Britain end the trade in slaves, a trade which had in theory already been abolished on previous occasions by Anglo-Portuguese agreement. Britain's interest was not so much to support Portugal as to keep France out of the Congo River by permitting it to become a Portuguese highway.

Opponents of the Anglo-Portuguese draft treaty rapidly mobilised their efforts. Leopold of the Belgians, whose private colonising association was active on the north bank of the river, had powerful friends in the British parliament and they were reluctant to approve the Portuguese treaty. Leopold also lobbied Paris, and eventually the opponents of Portugal gathered in Berlin in November 1884 to find a different solution to the Congo question. Portugal was allowed to have the south bank of the river but Leopold's 'association' was deemed to be a sovereign state and given control of the north bank. In compensation Portugal was granted an Atlantic enclave at Cabinda several miles north of the river mouth, a grant which was to have reverberating consequences in the twentieth century when petroleum was discovered there. The Berlin Conference unexpectedly carried over into the New Year and widened its agenda to decide how other disputes over colonial claims should be resolved without resort to armed conflict between European nations. This resolving of European disputes was, however, to be achieved without resort to the opinions and sensitivities of the African peoples whose legal, political and diplomatic rights were totally ignored in the ensuing European 'scramble' for land and labour. King Pedro V of Kongo ruled for another half-dozen years after the closing of the Berlin congress but it was his successors who paid the price for the decisions taken there.

One sequel to the Berlin Congress was the decision by the Baptist Missionary Society of Great Britain to establish a mission station in the Kongo royal capital. Unlike the Methodist mission, which Americans developed eastward out of Luanda, the Baptist mission had a sphere of influence which stretched northward across both banks of the Congo River and as far as Kinshasa. When British Baptist preachers arrived in San Salvador, the king's city, Angola's governor-general became so alarmed that he used a gun-boat to ferry a Catholic missionary up the coast to establish a rival mission. The Catholic initiative was not immediately followed up, however, and the Baptists became a dominant Christian influence in what became 'Portuguese Congo', the northern part of Angola. This arrival of a Baptist missionary society had deep repercussions for Angola's future. The urban focus of mission opportunity became Kinshasa, in the Belgian Congo, and in the first half of the twentieth century many Angolans migrated there in search of jobs and education. Those who remained behind in Angola suffered from the ever increasing labour demands of colonial enterprises. In particular the Portuguese logging companies in the forest enclave of Cabinda, north of the Congo River, were given the right to recruit ultra-cheap conscript workers from territory south of the river. Conditions in the logging camps were so oppressive, and the loss of labour on Kongo farms so painful, that in 1913 severe protests broke out. In an urgent search for a scape-goat the Portuguese blamed the Reverend J.S. Bowskill, a Baptist minister, for fomenting disloyalty to the colonial state, and locked him up, thus creating a diplomatic incident which reached the House of Commons in London. Conditions remained so oppressive that many Angolans migrated permanently across the border to work in the Belgian Congo. They became French-speakers, rather than Portuguese-speakers, and gained access to the clerical or craft training that was available under Belgian rule but rarely under Portuguese rule. The effects on northern Angola of the Belgian link, and of the Baptist presence, had lasting consequences throughout the twentieth century.

4

LAND AND LABOUR IN THE SOUTH

In the southern half of Angola a quasi-autonomous colony existed for some centuries with its own governor inhabiting a small palace in the dusty port city of Benguela which had been founded in 1617. The population around the city were semi-nomadic peoples who were dependent on their cattle and moved up and down the coast seeking fresh water and edible grasses. The city people were not only in-comers from all over the south who had either been brought there as slaves, or had sought opportunities to enhance their welfare by trading, but also migrants from the Portuguese enclaves as far north as Cabinda. The history of Benguela province in the nineteenth century was deeply affected by three phases of international commerce. The first, as in the north, was the opening up of the ivory trade in the 1830s, after which caravans penetrated ever deeper into the southern interior. The second, which evolved slowly from the 1870s, was a particularly profitable trade in wild rubber. And the third dimension was the revival of the old trade in workers, effectively slaves, who were shipped to the island of São Tomé no longer to grow coffee but now to grow cocoa. These three long-distance systems of trade generated other forms of economic production. Food for the caravans had to be grown, some of it in the environs of the city but much of it on the highland of the interior. Sugar also started to be cultivated, primarily to make rum which was a major trading commodity for the buying of ivory or rubber or slaves. A successful fishing industry affected the little out-ports of south Angola and provided dried protein for the colonial work force on the long merchant trails to the interior.

In 1848 the Hungarian trader Ladislaus Magyar moved his field of opera-tions from north Angola to south-central Angola. For health reasons he aban-doned the pestilential Congo valley for the salubrious highland behind Benguela. There he acquired an agricultural estate in a fertile valley in the kingdom of Bihé. To set up a trading business Magyar converted the money he had earned in five years of travelling the Atlantic shipping routes into suit-able merchandise for a trading expedition to the interior. His stock included 10,000 metres of cloth, 1,000 litres of brandy, twenty large barrels of gun-powder, three tons of salt, twenty rifles, and an assortment of shells, beads, mirrors and knives. His gold coin he kept for contingencies and emergencies. The cargo was made up into carefully checked, if heavy, loads and enough porters were hired to carry his thirty-six tons of stock. To reach the highland safely Magyar and his porters, with their caravan manager flying the Hungarian flag, joined a trading expedition returning home to Bihé which set out from Benguela in January 1849. The advance party consisted of 150 high-land hunters who acted as guards to clear the road ahead. A thousand porters carried Magyar's heavy loads and a thousand independent traders tagged along behind. The rear was secured by men with heavy 'rifles' who were slung about with cartridges. The weaponry not only provided protection but was also used to hunt game and provide the company with meat. When the caravan reached its destination, after forty days of up-hill marching, each porter was paid off with yards of cloth and bottles of brandy.

Once Magyar had chosen a site suitable for his trading compound he sent a carefully chosen diplomatic gift to the king of Bihé. This consisted of two red blankets, two flintlocks, two barrels of brandy, two kegs of gun-powder, 250 yards of cloth and 300 gun flints. He was thereupon invited to make a visit to the king's capital. This involved a slow ceremonial progress lasting several days. His retinue eventually wended its way through the city streets and past the many alleyways lined with thatched houses and curtained com-pounds. The power of the monarch was symbolised by the display of the skulls of enemies whom he had worsted and traitors whom he had executed. The town was divided by a stream which Magyar had to ford on the back of one of his slaves—to the great merriment of throngs of children. After the customary delays of protocol Magyar eventually reached the fearsome king's personal compound but was told that the king was 'busy' and could not see him until the next day. Eventually Magyar was invited to address the king's official lin-guist. An exchange of gifts took place and permission was granted for Magyar to settle permanently in the kingdom. The king even lent him a mule to carry him back to his newly-granted home. Magyar spent the next month building two stout walls around his compound, two houses in the European style, and fifty huts for his staff. In his domain he kept herds of cattle, sheep and goats and cultivated fields of maize and beans. His household consisted of thirty servants, some of them free men and others slaves whom he had bought. Some servants were former debt pawns who had bought their own freedom. Others were regular slaves who had been branded, like cattle, with their owner's property mark. Slaves, like livestock, had to be sheltered from thieves and prevented from straying. Magyar's slaves found it advantageous, however, to remain with a good owner who granted them a set of new clothes twice each year. Some of Magyar's male slaves married free women and therefore fathered free children. Several of his female slaves bore their master *mestizo* children in traditional colonial fashion. In the course of time the Bihé king became so pleased with his own 'white man' that he offered Magyar one of his forty-four daughters as a wedded bride. The fourteen-year-old princess was a cultured child whose grandmother had served as a high-status concubine in a near-by Brazilian household. At her wedding the little princess was not only decked out in fine clothes and hair beads but also wore a gold crucifix around her neck. Over the next years she bore Magyar five children and although only two survived to adulthood their descendants were still living on the coast at Benguela a hundred years later.

In the 1850s Magyar travelled widely on business, corresponded regularly with his father in Hungary, and even when on the remotest trading paths of eastern Angola kept up with world news through French and Brazilian newspapers delivered to him. The idea, peddled by later European adventurers, that Angola was a *terra incognita* at the heart of a dark continent was far from true. Communication with the outer world was slow, but it was regular. Magyar was able, in his surviving *magnum opus*, to provide a detailed account of all the kingdoms and principalities of the Ovimbundu highland. When he heard, on the efficient bush telegraph, that David Livingstone was travelling north from the Cape he set off towards the upper Zambezi to meet him. The surly Scotsman, however, was in no mood to meet a rival 'explorer'. Another important figure in this busy trading world was Magyar's young Portuguese neighbour, Silva Porto, but Livingstone disparagingly refused to meet him too. Silva Porto ran a successful trading empire for fifty years but Magyar himself was rather less successful. After one expedition Magyar had garnered a hundred lion skins and a huge haul of ivory but he was later attacked and robbed by rival traders. Soon after Magyar also lost his royal patron, his father-in-law, when a coup brought a jealous nephew to the throne of Bihé and Magyar had abruptly to leave the highland. He died in penury on the coast. His hope of sending the eldest son of his beloved princess to Hungary for his education never materialised. Magyar's father in Budapest tried to send his grandson 150 gold coins through one of the Benguela trading houses but the money never arrived.

Magyar's most famous neighbour, Silva Porto, was a Portuguese backwoodsman who had started as a book-keeper in Oporto, worked for a few years in Brazil, and then spent much of the rest of his long life as a caravan entrepreneur in the kingdom of Bihé. He arrived there in 1838. Two years before there had been a great rumpus when the king heard that Portugal intended to outlaw the buying of slaves. Portuguese traders had to flee from the highland. When they returned they brought temporary protection from the 'barbarities' of the fierce Bihé king in the form of a black militia commanded by a locally-born Portuguese Indian. The slave trade soon revived and within ten years there were reported to be one hundred 'Portuguese' traders in the kingdom, most of them black but a few of them *mestizo* or, in the case of Silva Porto, white. Some traders had hitherto supplied highland slaves to thirty-odd merchant houses in Luanda via the river port of Dondo. Silva Porto, however, used the long-distance path to Benguela and it was this trail which was adopted by Magyar. In return for slaves, traders regularly brought back commodities much in demand in the highland kingdoms: salt, rum, calico, gun-powder, and Belgian muskets from Liège or shot-guns, stamped with Victoria's crown, from Birmingham. When George Tams passed though Benguela in 1841 he estimated that 20,000 slaves were being illegally exported each year. Slaves became a standard unit of currency in Bihé and a ten-year-old child could be exchanged for a head-load of bees' wax. Although business flourished the traders felt insecure when they were at the mercy of kings engaged in their own fierce disputes, especially over questions of royal succession. Efforts to persuade the colonial government, down on the coast, to send an expensive military expedition to conquer Bihé and provide expatriates with security were all in vain. Trade nevertheless continued to expand and elephant tusks became so scarce that Silva Porto began seeking them in the far-off Zambezi territory. There the local Lozi king was not much interested in the assortment of trade goods which Angola could offer but he was interested in buying Angolan slaves to cultivate the farms on his great flood plain. Part of the slave trade was thus reversed and captives were herded east in exchange for ivory carried west. By the 1860s Silva Porto was even buying slaves from the Luba people of the upper Congo.

As the commercial networks reached ever further, they eventually overlapped the ivory and slave-trading networks based on Zanzibar. When East African traders, armed with guns, reached the upper Congo they established a kingdom of their own and elected one of their leaders, Msiri, as their king. One of this king's wives, Maria, came from Angola. When Leopold's armies of mercenaries closed in on the upper Congo Msiri was murdered and it was Maria's son who inherited his throne. This Angolan connection took on a more lasting dimension when a mission of Plymouth Brethren spread out along the trade paths which crossed the borderland between the Indian Ocean and the Atlantic. The Plymouth mission eventually became a significant feature of Angola's Christian tradition. In the meantime cross-continental trade continued to grow. As the world demand for ivory to make billiard balls, dominoes, piano keys and knife handles rose, international competition became ever more intense and merchants came all the way up from Cape Town to outbid the Angolans by offering better assortments of trade goods. They brought advanced Snyder firearms and even made payments in gold coin. To diversify their enterprises some highland entrepreneurs had once tried to grow cotton and benefit from the peak in cotton prices which briefly occurred during the American Civil War. When the war ended, and cotton prices fell, they hoped that rubber would be their salvation, though nothing quite matched the value of ivory.

The role of rubber in the economic evolution of Angola features in the work of a white Angolan sociologist from Benguela, Artur Pestana, who wrote classical novels under the *nom de plume* Pepetela. His book *Yaka* was named after the god-like mask with amber eyes who watched over the well-being of a trading family which ran a typical Portuguese store piled high with sacks of produce. Excitement came to Benguela town when the great caravans laden with rubber arrived down from the highland. Thousands of porters celebrated their safe return to the coast and money flowed with music and dancing and drinking. The good times did not last, however, and the great boom in rubber, which had accompanied the European proliferation of electric cables with rubber-coated insulation, collapsed early in the twentieth century. Wild rubber was replaced on the world market by plantation rubber from Brazil and Malaya. One proud fictional chief, arriving in Benguela with a huge haul of rubber, carried by his caravan of porters, was so shocked by the derisory price he was offered for his hard-won harvest that he publicly and dramatically set fire to all his latex bales rather than selling them at a loss. The wild rubber trade never did recover, though a later generation briefly sought to revive it during the Second World War when Japan conquered Malaya. Benguela store-keepers had meanwhile reverted to living on the margins of prosperity and diversifying their business as best they could.

Another focus of Portuguese activity on the Ovimbundu highland turned on the Luso-African town of Caconda. This district, a hundred miles inland from Benguela, probably had more 'civilised' settlers in the early twentieth century than the comparable Ambaca district in the hinterland of Luanda. The southern highland was healthier than the rest of Angola and the long-distance southern trade became ever more profitable. The export trade in *de facto* slaves to São Tomé was active but there were also a series of attempts to use purchased labourers inside the colony. A number of absentee São Tomé plantation owners in Lisbon thought that they could buy large tracts of land around Caconda and use local slaves to plant tropical crops without the expense, or the political hazard, of taking them to their estates on the island. This São Tomé initiative was less than successful but colonisation on the Caconda lands took on a wholly new and unexpected dimension when Dutch-speaking immigrants began to infiltrate the district. The South African Boers, hitherto settled in the far south of Angola, began to move into the Caconda district with their retainers and bought slaves to serve as relatively expensive farm labourers and as wagon drovers. The cost of slaves had risen when the search for rubber had penetrated ever deeper into the interior and had required longer columns of porters to bring produce to the coast. Porters from remote lands were, moreover, not always available to local employers and many finished up on schooners, or steamers, which took them off to São Tomé after they had put an unwitting thumb-print on a labour contract.

In the midst of all this activity the district commissioner at Caconda tried to live a lifestyle he deemed to be compatible with his status. Porters coming up from the coast brought him crystal glasses from which to drink his champagne and a fully sprung mattress for his bed. The invoices for his domestic purchases listed foreign plates, bowls, tureens, butter dishes and water pitchers, as well as fancy coffee pots, teapots, china cups, wine glasses and three decanters for brandy. Such extravagance compared sharply with the more usual imports consisting of drums of cooking oil, boxes of dried cod fish, metal cans of lamp oil, and kegs of red wine. Meat was surprisingly scarce on the highland and 'civilised' Angolans—white and black—preferred dried salt-fish imported from Europe even when living in the deepest interior. Bread was a luxury and imported wheat was alleged to be almost as expensive as salt, head-loaded up from the drying pans at Benguela. High living had a long history among the élite citizens of Angola but the cost of hiring skilled porters who could carry fragile loads up the escarpment to the highland was exorbitant.

The task of a self-important commissioner was essentially that of a district magistrate and a tax inspector. He was supported by a 'professor', a doctor, a nurse, a judge, and a ferry master. He spent municipal money maintaining the prison, lighting the main street, and hosting music festivals. The Caconda district even had a school run by a Catholic mission. The campus was an hour's walk out of town but, although secluded, lonely male settlers nevertheless clustered round the girls' dormitory like bees round a honey pot. The school catered for 200 children, some of them Boers and *mestizos*. The district as a whole apparently had a population of about 3,000 *mestizo*, white, black, and Indian 'Portuguese'. Caconda also allegedly had about 40,000 African 'hearths' on which hut-taxes could be imposed. Tax collectors found it expedient, however, to minimise the census returns on taxable subjects since they were afraid of penetrating, unless accompanied by armed soldiers, into villages beyond the environs of the city. A reduced hut-tax roll may also have enhanced their opportunities for making undeclared illegal profits. The unreliability of the census figures became particularly notorious at election time. In 1884 309 votes were registered, in 1901 the number had risen to 1,439, but in 1894 over six thousand ballot papers had allegedly been cast though they were hastily burnt before they could be checked. The votes were always for the absentee candidate nominated by Lisbon. No votes ever seem to have been cast in Caconda for an opposition candidate, or for a local dignitary.

The Caconda commissioner had particular difficulty in recruiting 'native militias' needed to hunt down robbers, such as the ones who looted the forty-nine-man caravan which brought the imperial consul of Germany on a visit to Caconda in 1900. The garrison at Caconda consisted of fewer than a hundred soldiers and fifty militiamen. When it came to protecting the district from Kwanyama raiders, who came up from the south, the commissioner depended on the Boer community for protection. In return he gave them licences to hold modern rifles, even Martini-Henry ones, and also the right to keep as booty any cattle they captured during their campaigns. In addition to the problem of security, questions relating to bribery regularly exercised the authorities. When a 'native chief' brought a gift pig to the commissioner it generated an extensive correspondence over legal malpractice. The bigger law cases facing a magistrate, however, were the ones concerning the ownership of slaves. Slaves who ran away from brutal masters or mistresses were soundly thrashed at the town pillory before being unquestioningly returned to their owners. If justice were to be sought by an African he or she was better advised to approach one of the missions in the district for help.

A very rare insight into the nature of Angolan slavery by one of its victims turned up unexpectedly when the autobiography of a young Angolan was unearthed in the Swiss archive of a Basel Mission station in Cameroun. Salomo Paipo was enlisted for plantation service at the turn of the century in a village some miles north of Caconda.

> Our town was in a peaceful grassland and was open to all traders. One day a party of Portuguese arrived and asked our headman if they might recruit workers. To facilitate the deal they gave him a dash of various kinds of brandy and some beautiful textiles. They explained that any recruit would be given a free passage home after two years' service, and thus the headman called out 'whoever wants to sign up for labour duty should step forward'. Several of us boys, Kolombo, Ngondja, Kaloko, came forward as did many adults who were willing to follow the recruiting agents. While we got ready the white men purchased cattle, sheep, goats, pigs and hens which our herdsmen offered to drive to the coast. At the beach a clerk took our names and we then loaded all the livestock on board a tramp steamer. We also loaded potatoes, onions, corn, rubber and palm kernels. Once the ship had weighed anchor we were all inoculated and our clothes were sprayed with strong disinfectant. The next day we steamed amid canon salutes into Luanda harbour and the livestock was unloaded. We then sailed on to Cabinda where the traders who came aboard spoke the pidgin English of Liberian Kru Boys and sold a quantity of ducks. An interpreter enabled me to buy some dried cassava for the voyage. Twenty-four hours later we anchored off the beautiful island of São Tomé which has many fine brick-and-tile houses. Here we were lowered into a dingy and rowed ashore. The island seemed covered in pineapples, coconuts, melons, oil-palms, cocoa trees and coffee plantations.

This peaceful and optimistic autobiographical account of labour recruitment in southern Angola is in sharp contrast with the eyewitness description of a travelling journalist who crossed the same region a short while afterwards, in 1906. Henry Nevinson wrote a series of articles on 'a modern slavery' for *Harper's Magazine*. His account was one of violent kidnapping rather than material inducement. Héli Chatelain saw copies of *Harper's Magazine* and wrote discreetly to his friends to say that they seemed to be accurate in every particular. Two years later, when William Cadbury walked up the recruitment trail from the coast, he too saw evidence of a much more violent side to the labour recruitment than that revealed by the Basel document. He found discarded wooden shackles piled up at the side of the path. They had been removed from captives who had been marched down to the coast from the far interior and who had only been unshackled so that they could sign labour contracts as though they were free men and women. This was a far cry from the account of the carefree village lads who had signed up with Salomo a short while before. Violent methods of recruitment were not the only problem which the people of southern Angola faced and the question of the working conditions on the islands to which they were taken also became very controversial. The Cadbury report said that the island work schedules were not too severe, the diet was apparently adequate, and the better plantations had infirmaries to tend the sick workers who had been expensively imported from the mainland. Indentured labour practices were no worse than those applied to the Indian and Chinese 'coolies' who kept the British Empire turning. One feature, however, was unacceptable to a philanthropic cocoa buyer: the lack of any tradition of repatriation. Salomo had been promised a contract of two years but most *serviçais* were enlisted for five years. But at the end of five years, Cadbury complained, the workers were automatically signed up for another five-year term, and then another, and another, so that none of the highland recruits from Caconda and elsewhere ever returned home. This, said Cadbury, amounted to slavery and unless repatriation were to be introduced to the island regime he and his fellow chocolate manufacturers would cease buying Portuguese cocoa beans.

Salomo would not have agreed with Cadbury's assessment that working conditions on the beautiful plantations were acceptable by the norms of late Victorian imperialism. His description of life on São Tomé contrasts sharply with his light-hearted account of the journey to the island. Work, he said, was a constant torment. Labouring began at dawn and did not cease till the noon-day lunch bell rang. The afternoon shift carried on till nightfall. Living quarters for horses and oxen were better than those for the men and women who gathered the harvest or for the child workers who sorted the fruits. Far from appreciating the infirmaries which were proudly shown to visiting dignitaries, Salomo reported that any worker who claimed to be ill was accused of shirking and was whipped until the blood flowed. One of Salomo's companions was so severely beaten that he hanged himself. Furious planters refused to grant him a dignified burial but had his corpse incinerated on the public highway. Had Salomo remained a plantation worker he felt sure he too would have died, but by good fortune he was taken on as an apprentice by a carpenter who travelled round the island doing house repairs. Since his master liked to take long lunch breaks, and to indulge in competitive ninepin bowling with his mates, the apprentice had lighter working conditions and shorter hours than his fellow Angolans. Soon, however, a dour and violent new labour agent arrived and when indentured men asked when they would be allowed to go home the agent became so angry that indenture became slavery, as Cadbury said. Salomo solved his predicament by stealing a boat and allowing the Atlantic currents to drift him, over ten hungry and thirsty days, to the coast of German Kamerun where he was rescued by villagers, taken to the Swiss mission, given an education, and trained as a school master who could write an autobiography.

Salomo left his native Caconda at much the same time as English adventurers arrived to roam across the plateau and beyond. One of the most remarkable Englishmen who explored Angola early in the twentieth century was a big-game hunter, Major Percy Powell-Cotton. He employed the world's most skilled taxidermists and set up an astonishing diorama of stuffed animals, ranging from elephants to aardvarks, all in a naturalistic African setting, on his family estate in Kent. The rarest of his specimens was the Giant Sable Antelope from Angola. During the Angolan civil wars of the 1990s it was feared that the last of these majestic beasts had been eaten by famished guerrillas but when a possible survivor was found the ministry of tourism attempted to match its DNA with that of the major's specimen. In the 1930s the daughters of the family returned to Africa and used their skills as amateur anthropologists to study the customs of Angola's people. They bought an old pick-up truck, loaded it with salt from the Benguela salt pans, and—to the astonishment of local settlers who had never before seen women drivers capable of keeping an old motor running on their sandy trails—set off to explore the highland. At each village they offered a bag of salt for permission to use their ciné camera to film initiation rituals and dances as well as weddings and funerals. They were also interested in arts and crafts and filmed the beating of bark-cloth and the smelting of iron ore. They filled their truck with every type of carving, pottery and basket-work which they brought home to expand their father's diorama into one of the best of Angola's small ethnographic museums, much visited by later generations of children and tourists in Kent. Some of their exhibits they gave to the Pitt-Rivers Museum in Oxford.

Powell-Cotton was not the only turn-of-the-century Englishman to venture into the deep interior of Angola. One army captain, who had served the British in the Anglo-Boer war, penetrated as far as Kasanje, 300 miles north of Caconda, but was murdered in a petty squabble over the price a butcher wanted to charge him for a goat. Other Britons, geologists, prospectors and miners, combed the district for opportunities but caused much distress at the religious missions by buying slaves to do their digging and staff their households. The main witness to these events was Héli Chatelain who spent ten years on the highland after the self-sufficient, and very evangelical, Taylor mission which he had helped to found had failed in the hinterland of Luanda. Chatelain's new mission, established on the Caconda highland, aspired—like the Taylor mission—to be self-reliant with minimal dependence on Swiss church subsidies. The mission ran an important highland store, established a pharmacy, set up a bank, built a saw-mill and operated a granary with its own water-driven corn-mill. It did business with all the expatriate communities of the highland and hired out its artisans and carpenters. Although Chatelain approved of new business enterprises he strongly disapproved of the moral climate which came in their wake. His store maintained a strict prohibition on the selling of tobacco and snuff, to which the African population was becoming addicted, and also refused to trade in alcoholic spirits from which old-style traders earned a large share of their profit. The most important British enterprise from which Chatelain hoped to gain a benefit was the building of the railway up from Benguela. To his dismay, however, the route eventually chosen did not pass through Caconda but went further north, to the African town of Bihé where Magyar and Silva Porto had once been the great caravan masters. Relations between the Swiss missionary and the railway engineers deteriorated when Chatelain visited the building site. He tried to protest about the labour conditions that he witnessed. The British consul-general in Angola came to inspect progress on the line but refused to meet Chatelain. The concessionaire was hiring Indian 'coolies' on indentured contracts to build the line because they were cheaper than African navvies. They were also less likely to flee from the building sites into the unknown African wilderness. Chatelain's main objective in Africa was to improve labour conditions but the British consul was quite unwilling to recognise that many Indians were dying of starvation and fever. The railway's use of indentured labour from India severely limited any moral high ground which Britain might have used to protest about the Portuguese trade in indentured workers for their cocoa islands.

The Swiss mission which Héli Chatelain created had arrived in Caconda in 1897. At the time an international conference was held in Brussels to revitalise the world campaign against slavery. This crusade appealed to Chatelain and he devoted the rest of his life to campaigning against slavery. He gained support from American philanthropists and when he established his new mission station on the highland he called it Lincoln after the president who had outlawed slavery in the United States. The Swiss anti-slavery league which sponsored him was run by his sister and was loosely connected to the Presbyterian Free Church in Lausanne. The mission eventually flourished for a hundred years but in its first ten years it went through severe difficulties. The Caconda commissioner claimed that it was not a mission at all but a common trading venture. The Union Castle shipping line agreed and, although the Swiss bookstore was the official agent for the British and Foreign Bible Society, the mission workers were refused the discount which the shipping company granted to *bona fide* preachers seeking berths. The Swiss recruits themselves were a bit surprised that Chatelain, who in his youth had been a keen singer of Methodist hymns, did not insist that his workshop staff take part in religious services. He seemed more devoted to wagon trading than to proselytising. The mission wagon, with a full team of eighteen oxen, travelled through the villages selling an assortment of goods such as might have been found in the seasonal fair of any Swiss village. The heavy commodities were sugar, salt, cooking oil and soap but in addition Chatelain sold padlocks, door-locks, pen-knives, brass nails, shirt buttons, rings, belts, kerchiefs, hats, gun-flints, paper, mirrors, needles, matches, mouth-organs and bracelets. The supply of wagons, especially for Boer customers, became a key part of the mission business plan. Chatelain corresponded with the Illinois firm of Studebaker, which built great wagons for the American plains, and explained that the ones needed in Africa had to be very rugged, and to have chain harnesses for twice as many oxen as those used on the American prairies. Although the Boers depended on Chatelain for the supply, and maintenance, of their wagons they deeply resented his interference in their domestic affairs and especially in their treatment of their slaves. This resentment was echoed by the district commissioner of Caconda and his Portuguese settlers who also used slaves extensively. Eventually, by a piece of chicanery which brought in the governor-general while avoiding a diplomatic incident, the commissioner managed to have Chatelain expelled from his highland. He accused the mission of failing to fill in a tax return on liquor sales, a commodity which, as everyone knew, was emphatically not traded by the mission store. Many Caconda residents who owed the Swiss bank money cheered at Chatelain's departure and some would even have liked to burn the mission down and destroy all its financial records. To get away safely Chatelain sought the help of a distinguished Catholic priest, Mathias Delgado. Chatelain himself died in 1908 but for the next thirty years Delgado carried on his friend's work on African languages. He eventually became a professor of Bantu language studies and edited two volumes of the great history of the Angolan wars which had been written in the

1680s by Cadornega, an old Jewish scholar who had lived out his days in African exile after his mother had been sentenced to be burnt at the stake on the main Lisbon square for practising Hebrew worship.

In the last years of the nineteenth century politicians in Lisbon were increasingly exercised over problems of empire. Portugal had long aspired to extend its Atlantic territory across Angola to Mozambique, an ambition which inevitably brought it into conflict with Britain. In 1878 a Portuguese army officer, Major Serpa Pinto, had crossed south Angola from Benguela to the Lozi Kingdom before heading down to Pretoria and Durban. He published his two volumes of travels in London and was later sent to Mozambique where he sought to acquire Lake Malawi for Portugal, thereby wrong-footing both the British prime minister, Lord Salisbury, and the maverick entrepreneur, Cecil Rhodes. Missionaries brandishing the Scottish name of Livingstone, claimed the lake for themselves and Salisbury dared not offend Scottish sensibilities. In Cape Town Rhodes claimed possession of the gold-bearing regions inland of Mozambique and used financial inducements from his diamond mines to buy support for his actions in both British houses of parliament. Thus it was that when Portugal laid claim to a cross-continental swathe of Africa, Lord Salisbury found it expedient 'mildly' to remonstrate. His ultimatum of January 1890, banning Portugal from claiming territory along the middle stretch of the Zambezi, may have seemed mild to him but to the Portuguese it was a dagger in the back wielded by their oldest ally. It caused an uproar, the effects of which lasted for a generation. The future of Angola as the Atlantic gateway to the whole of Central Africa crumbled. Portugal's inability to counteract such rampant British imperialism brought traders such as Silva Porto to despair. In April 1890 the disillusioned old man wrapped himself in the Portuguese flag, sat on a barrel of gun-powder, and lit the fuse. The explosion reverberated around the Portuguese empire.

5

FROM SLAVE TRADING TO WHITE SETTLEMENT

The year 1890 was probably the most important turning point in the modern history of Angola. The British 'ultimatum', which limited Portuguese expansion to the east, transformed the course of Portuguese imperial history. The dream of a New Brazil, comparable in size to the independent Brazilian empire, or even comparable to the United States, died at the hands of Lord Salisbury. The trauma felt in Lisbon was profound. Portugal had already lost the north bank of the Congo River to King Leopold. The southern frontier of a prospective Central African 'empire' was being encroached upon by German advances in Namibia. Now Portugal's oldest ally, Britain, had vetoed any Angolan expansion eastward. The dream of a rose-coloured map stretching from sea to shining sea had been shot down in one diplomatic dispatch. In British diplomatic history the ultimatum of 1890 does not even merit a footnote. Salisbury's 'mild remonstration' was deemed to be of no particular significance. In Portugal it heralded the end of the old colonial order. The African empire, which had become the guarantor of Portugal's status as a world power, was now at risk and had been cut back to the trading hinterland of coastal enclaves in Angola and Mozambique. Even these territories were no longer secure. In the east Cecil Rhodes helped to finance the creation of the private Mozambique Company which limited Portuguese sovereignty until 1940. Rhodes also built the Mozambique railway to Rhodesia. A 'red' map along the mythical highway from Cairo to the Cape cut a great swathe through the 'pink' map which the great Portuguese explorers had aspired to create. Angola was even at risk of being dismembered altogether when in 1898

Britain engaged in secret diplomatic negotiations with Germany. The abortive deal would have granted Luanda province to Britain and allowed Germany a free commercial reign in the rest of the territory.

When news of the British veto on the joining of Angola to Mozambique reached Luanda the authorities desperately set about trying to limit the damage. A dynamic young army officer, half Portuguese and half Irish, happened to be visiting the little plateau communities of Angola's deep south when he received an urgent coded telegram ordering him to report immediately to Silva Porto's trading station at Bihé on the Benguela highland. Paiva Couceiro arrived in Bihé shortly before old man Silva Porto, the legendary trader and explorer, lit the fuse on his barrel of gunpowder, killing himself and thereby shaking the whole Portuguese empire into diplomatic action. The young officer assembled a few dozen soldiers, a minimal number of bearers, and set off to claim all the territory he could reach along the western tributaries of the Zambezi in what was to become the Angolan province of Kwando-Kubango. Over the next few years Paiva Couceiro became one of the best-informed voices of Portuguese imperial ambition and in 1907 he was appointed governor-general of Angola. His vision of a future in which Angola would cease to be primarily a slave-exporting market colony and become a settler colony for white immigrants was one that would be carried forward by another dynamic young soldier, Norton de Matos, in 1912–15 and 1921–24. Before the new era of settler colonialism dawned, however, Central Africa went through great turbulence. Angola became engulfed in a storm over slavery that shook the colonial world. In Congo the crisis had been triggered by the brutal attempts of Leopold's men to generate revenue to cover the cost of running a private enterprise colonial administration. The storm led in 1908 to the confiscation of Leopold's 'Congo State' by the government of Belgium. In Angola the crisis arose out of the on-going sale of indentured workers for the cocoa islands. Indirectly it undermined the Saxe-Coburg monarchy in Portugal and in 1908 led to the assassination of King Carlos. The Portuguese king was succeeded by his young son, Manuel, but two years later he was overthrown by revolutionaries. The last monarchical ruler of Portugal fled into exile in England. This Portuguese mutiny, which was started by the *carbonari*, working-class Lisbon anarchists, was subsequently captured by middle-class Freemasons, who headed a new, liberal, republican regime.

One of the most bizarre consequences of republican liberalism, designed to strengthen a white settler presence in the Portuguese colonies, was the attempt in 1912 to create a 'homeland' for Jews in Angola. Paulo Dias, a grandson of the navigator Bartholomew Dias, was a Jewish coloniser who became lord-proprietor of Angola in 1571. He brought Jewish artisans to Luanda in the hope of building profitable wind-mills to replace the traditional pounding of corn in mortars. Portuguese persecution led more Jews to emigrate in the seventeenth century. Despite a recurrent confrontation between state and synagogue the empire always required Jewish financial and administrative skills as well as engineering ones. In seventeenth-century Angola it was suspected that one 'chief factor' responsible for the management of the royal taxes was a clandestine rabbi who conducted services in a secret Luanda synagogue. By the late eighteenth century emigration had become more open and a Jewish heritage was recorded in the river port of Dondo where Zagury Street and Bensaude Street heralded a golden age. After 1910 the new republican regime proposed massively to increase the number of Jews in Angola by inviting in not only Iberian settlers but also a far wider range of migrants from the beleaguered ghettos of eastern Europe. An attempt had been made in 1905 to found a Jewish homeland in the British 'protectorate' of Uganda but it had come to nothing. A 'protectorate' guaranteed the welfare of native peoples and offered little to attract white settlers. Angola, by contrast, was a 'conquest colony' and so 'native interests' could be disregarded and imperial interests could become paramount.

The plan for a Jewish homeland in Angola was developed over several years by Israel Zangwill, a British-born Russian novelist who chaired a Jewish Territorial Organisation with offices on Portugal Street in London. In 1897 Zangwill had visited Palestine and deemed it unsuitable for a Jewish homeland since it was dry, rocky and filled with indigenous inhabitants. He was advised by 'experts' that Angola was the finest part of Africa for a settler colony since it had a temperate climate, well-watered agricultural land, a high plateau, and above all scarcely any 'native' inhabitants. Zangwill naturally queried the reference to the scantiness of the native population, but was assured that there were no more than 200,000 natives on a highland as large as England. It gradually emerged that this mendacious advice came from an engineer on the Benguela Railway who had not been able to recruit African navvies and so had been tempted to rely on Indian coolies instead. What the engineer wanted above all, however, was to attract hard-working white settlers who would establish an agricultural colony along his highland route and thus enhance traffic on his railway. The proposal was enthusiastically backed by the Jewish community on the Witwatersrand gold mines and by Jews on the Congo copper belt. It was assumed that the railway's all-powerful financier,

57

Robert Williams, would welcome the scheme. Land was cheap on the Angolan highland and a surprising enthusiasm emanated from Portugal, which thought that Jewish settlers would open up the high country and show that it was under 'effective occupation' and could not therefore be claimed to be 'vacant' by Germany or Britain.

A bill to facilitate the creation of a Jewish colony was presented to the Portuguese parliament on 20 June 1912. It specified that all Jewish settlers would be required to become Portuguese subjects. They would be granted land concessions and permitted to build schools, hospitals and 'edifices of public utility'. It gradually became clear, however, that there were problems with the legislation, problems that were to illuminate the future history of white colonisation in Angola. It was pointed out that land grants of 250 hectares could not be worked by settlers alone without the recruiting of native labour. Settlers would, moreover, be expected to provide their own tools and investment capital. A Jewish colonisation society would have, at its own expense, to build highways, bridges, sewers, irrigation works and canals. Each immigrant would be expected to obey existing laws restricting mining, quarrying, forestry, hunting and fishing. Failure adequately to develop each individual concession within two years would lead to its confiscation by the state together with any improvements that had been made on the land. Naturalisation papers would be issued, for the price of one US dollar, to all heads of settler families on the specific condition that they were not, like so many Portuguese immigrants, either criminals or convicts. One requirement of naturalisation was that all Jewish children should be taught exclusively in the Portuguese language and would become liable to Portuguese military service. The almost absurd optimism behind the scheme was partially punctured by a Scottish professor of geography who was of the opinion that only the most desperate of economic refugees would choose to settle in Angola. Without mining rights, he said, even a family with a quarter of a square mile of territory would not be able to survive. Despite the cautious warnings Israel Zangwill visited Lisbon, met the newly-appointed governor-general, Norton de Matos, sought advice from Dr Bensaude of the Lisbon Technical Institute, and gained assurances from a Mr Levy that Portuguese Jews would establish a support committee for the Angolan venture. In London, by contrast, all attempts to obtain backing for Angolan colonisation failed in spite of dropping the names of Lord Rothschild, of Sir Harry Johnston, the great Central African treaty-maker, of Henry Nevinson, the anti-slavery campaigner, and even of young Winston Churchill. It was in Lisbon, however, that serious opposition broke out.

Portugal, it turned out, wanted individual settlers as colonists, not an ideological scheme to create a Jewish homeland, a new Zion such as the one promised in Palestine by Britain four years later. The problem was compounded when Zangwill realised that anti-clerical republicans would insist that colonists should not be allowed any religious education or the dissemination of Jewish practices so vital to survival. The scheme collapsed and when, a few years later, Catholic nationalists took control of the Portuguese empire, being Jewish became a handicap though covert loyalty to Portugal's Hebrew inheritance nevertheless survived. A leading dealer in Angolan diamonds conducted his business in Luanda with a Jewish opposite number from Johannesburg. When, in retirement, the elderly Portuguese broker died, his Catholic wife was astonished to read in his will that he had always been a secret Jew and that he would like his old trading partner from Johannesburg to attend his funeral in Lisbon and read a Jewish prayer of mourning over his coffin.

Two years after the Portuguese revolution of 1910, and in the year of the collapse of the Jewish colonising project, Norton de Matos started the first of his two terms as the energetic governor-general of Angola. He was later to become a giant figure in Portuguese politics, commanding an expeditionary force sent to Flanders during the First World War, becoming master of Portugal's grand lodge of Freemasons, presiding over the League of Nations in Geneva, and standing as opposition candidate for the presidency of Portugal during the forty-year dictatorship of Salazar. As the most dynamic of all Angola's governors, Norton introduced authoritarian decrees aimed at making the colony at least economically self-reliant, if not actually profitable for the mother country. His concepts of development, like those of the British and the French, inherited some of the nineteenth-century racist and sexist prejudices of old colonial ideologues but with an expectation that Africans would play a positive if subsidiary role in the new republican empire. The great ideologue of empire in late nineteenth-century Portugal had been Oliveira Martins. Martins claimed that 'documents show that the Negro is an inferior anthropological specimen better described as anthropoid rather than human'. At the height of Social Darwinism Martins thought that the idea of educating Negroes was absurd in view of their lack of mental capacity. The racism he propounded was matched by an equally virulent sexism. African women were said by their detractors to be hedonistic vixens who used their sensuality and obscene traditions to corrupt European men. Norton inherited some of these prejudices and decreed that any colonial official in the Angolan provinces should no longer establish a *ménage* with his black housekeeper but should instead marry a white wife. Surviving concepts of Social Darwinism preserved a hostility to mixed-race children, and Norton aspired to replace Angola's old mixed-race élites with a new generation of white Portuguese immigrants. This racism had adverse effects on the Creole élites of Luanda, Ambaca, and the old colonial towns. The new carpet-baggers to whom the republic promised white-collar jobs in the colonies were particularly hostile to black and brown Angolans who had the training and experience which semi-literate white settlers did not possess.

Portuguese governments had long debated the possibility of encouraging white immigration to Angola but decided on balance that sending immigrants to Brazil, from where they could post cash remittances back home, would be more beneficial. After the revolution of 1910 the concept of free white immigration revived and by 1920 the white population of Angola had risen from 12,000 to 20,000. Norton gradually realised, however, that his ability to bring about real change was limited. White settlers would not come to Angola unless they were supplied with cheap labourers. The old white nuclei of the far south, Pernambuco refugees, Madeira peasants, and Algarve fishermen, survived but in the 1920s the Boer communities packed their great wagon-loads of possessions on to lorries and returned to the now independent Union of South Africa. An attempt to replace Boers with Portuguese orphans as apprentice farmers failed. Equally struggling were the initial attempts to get Portuguese migrants to settle on the Ovimbundu highland in the manner previously proposed for Eastern European Jews.

Norton argued that he could only create a white colony if white women as well as white men were willing to become settlers. Social life for a white housewife in the bush was, however, harsh and lonely, with opportunities for gossip limited to conversations with the odd itinerant trader who might pass by on the sandy trails every week or two. The concept of white family life appeared more viable in towns than in the countryside and so a new, segregated, city was planned for Portuguese settlers in the old highland kingdom of Huambo. Colonial dreamers spoke of a New Lusitania as they planned the colonial city. Even the promise of *apartheid*, the segregation of white peasants and black peasants, did not attract many, and those who were given subsidised ocean passages sometimes finished up as unemployed vagrants wishing to go home. The offer of a fifteen-year mortgage, a one-hundred-hectare farm, and the loan of plough-oxen, was not enough to attract farmers. The optimistic vision of health workers, of educational missions, of cadres of technicians, of 'secular priests' to raise the moral standards of illiterate white peasants, was insufficient to stimulate immigration. Norton had failed to realise that little of Angola's vast territory had the soil fertility or rainfall to make farming viable. He also failed to see that the most productive soils were already occupied by indigenous populations. When immigrants did arrive, conflict between white land-hunters and black land-losers became endemic.

One place where white settlers tried to establish an agricultural colony was a small plateau behind the coastal town of Old Benguela, re-named Porto Amboim. Resistance by peasants growing their subsistence crops in the fertile valleys was fierce in 1904 and 1907, and in 1917 the settlers and their assimi-lated associates were killed or driven out, while their plantation houses were burnt down. Similar murderous protests took place at the same time in the neighbouring district of Selles. When the settlers returned, with an armed force of some 1,000 soldiers, they found the plateau virtually abandoned and to re-establish their palm stands and their coffee groves they had to recruit reluctant labour from inland. Unlettered Portuguese immigrants from the rough hills of northern Portugal were brought in and taught the art of estate management on 100 small plantations. The poor white managers supervised black bailiffs who summoned the work teams to the fields with the great plan-tation bell which rang out in the cold dawn and regulated the routine. The heavy work of humping sacks of coffee beans was undertaken by porters recruited from the kingdom of Bailundu. Weeding, pruning and harvesting were done by the unskilled conscripts. Relaxation was sometimes provided on the occasion of an important funeral, and on the birthday of a white landlord a Sunday dance might be held in the district. So valuable was Amboim coffee that Norton de Matos authorised the building of a little railway which eventu-ally reached the groves and was served by four steam engines, sixteen goods wagons and two passenger coaches. The colony was taking root when in 1929 the world financial markets crashed. Poverty struck the planters and hunger struck the workers who had become dependent on maize bought by their employers from the interior. Settlers sought new markets for sugar, for sisal and even for cassava but all agricultural production required the cheapest possible supply of labour. Employers complained bitterly that thousands of Angolans were fleeing the colony to seek better conditions and wages in Congo and Namibia.

Three years before the Wall Street crash, a new regime was established in Portugal when Catholic army officers toppled the republic of the Freemasons. The army was incapable of managing Portugal's money and so it invited António Salazar, a part-time Catholic journalist with a Coimbra degree in book-keeping, misleadingly known as 'economics', and who had once been appointed to a temporary lectureship in financial law, to become its minister for finance. Salazar accepted, but only on condition that the army should give him supreme power. He thereupon cut government expenditure, including colonial expenditure, to the bone and spared only the army's own budget. A colonial act was passed which effectively reversed Norton's vision of a colony based on the self-reliant labour of hard-working white peasants. The new plan recognised that the only highland production of real worth was the cultivation of maize and beans by ultra-cheap African plantation workers. Instead of becoming toiling sons of the soil, the next generation of settlers would become shop-keepers. Towns would become service centres in which artisans would make the consumer goods aspired to by a modestly-prospering white working class and its middle-class managers. Critics protested that such colonisation would drain Portugal's scarce supply of teachers and technicians and bitterly pointed out that the empty lands of North America and Australia had been successfully colonised by convicts, desperadoes and adventurers. New settlers who arrived in Angola were only very modestly qualified but they nevertheless rose up the social scale by employing cheap black workers recruited for them by local district commissioners. As 'New Lisbon' grew in Huambo, black peasants from the countryside came into the notionally segregated town as choppers of wood, as haulers of water, and as scullery maids. A few domestic servants lived inside the white city but many more dwelt in the growing suburbs. There they built thatched houses in traditional style and lived much as they would have done in their villages, with poor roads and no sanitation. The least successful of the white immigrants also settled in these rough slums and walked daily into town to find workshop employment. Segregation was far from complete but both black and white communities were acutely aware that whiteness provided a status that could be materially beneficial however poor one's level of skill or education. A major employer of both black and white labour was the Benguela railway.

The new regime continued to advocate racial separation until the 1950s when its spin-doctors endorsed, in theory at least, the Brazilian concept of 'Lusotropicalism'. This ideology praised the openness of the Portuguese who, it proclaimed, mixed freely, both culturally and conjugally, with other races, without any prejudice. Reality, however, was rather different. Portuguese society protected the virginity of white women almost as ferociously as Islamic society protected its women. This protection did not extend, however, to black women. The female victims of empire continued to carry *mestizo* children fathered by their employers, or by the promiscuous sons of their employers, but these children were all too often dismissed as black. The distinction between the theory and practice of race relations in mid-twentieth-century Angola was vividly displayed in the writings of Castro Soromenho, a Mozambican author of Indian descent who lived and worked in rural Angola. The 1930s community described in his novel *Terra Morta* was located 300 miles beyond the terminus of the Ambaca railway. The district commissioner had a white wife, Dona Jovita, in the style commended by Norton de Matos, but as the only white woman for miles around she was very lonely. The half-dozen white men, traders and clerks, could socialise with one another and met together each evening on the wide verandas of their bungalows to play cards and smoke cigars. They engaged freely in gossip, remembering the suffocating restrictions of Portugal, where every other person might be a police informer. They dreamt of the rich coffee lands of Brazil to which they hoped one day to emigrate. These men felt the loneliness of their remote posting too, and the arrival of a motor car, or merchant lorry, along the muddy trail from the railway was a great event. Later in the evening, when his drinking companions had retired for the night, and extinguished their hurricane lanterns, a man sometimes assuaged his loneliness by discreetly ordering one of the sepoys, who guarded the prison with their muzzle-loading muskets, to bring a young female prisoner to the bungalow bedroom. The girl had to steal herself to tolerate the strange, foul, smell of a white man. Some of the prisoners were women who had been rounded up in the villages which supplied workers to the diamond fields. They were held hostage until men who had escaped from the mine compounds were compelled to return to work. In the dusty little town a significant proportion of the servile population were described as 'mulattoes'.

Another fictional insight into the racial attitudes of twentieth-century Angola can be gained from the early work of Ralph Delgado, the son of one of the first colonial commissioners to govern the old kingdom of Bihé. In 1935, before he became one of Angola's leading historians, Delgado wrote a novel on love in the tropics. This featured a young colonial bachelor who arrived from Lisbon in the harbour city of Benguela. His work schedule as an accountant seemed very flexible. The local bureaucracy employed numbers of clerks who supervised the customs house and registered in great ledgers every single sack of potatoes or bundle of garden hoes that came into the colony. The new arrival spent much of his time with other young white lads drinking beer in the numerous bars. The town boasted an electric theatre which showed romantic films and it also had a dance hall. The young immigrant shuddered, however, when he realised that his new colonial friends did not recoil from dancing with black girls. But loneliness gradually eroded his puritanical sentiments and he found himself slyly admiring the young *mestizo* daughter of one of the grand Benguela households. He began regularly to promenade down the avenue below her balcony on Sunday afternoons. Eventually he met her at a society ball and even persuaded himself that he might bring himself to marry her. But fate intervened, ill-health forced him to return to Portugal, and his horrified family rapidly married him off to a socially acceptable white bride.

It might have been expected that the staunchly Catholic regime of the 1930s in Portugal would advantage Catholics in Angola, but relations between an authoritarian state and the church were not always easy. Salazar had been known in his home village as Father António since he had once taken the minor vows in a tentative, but abortive, step towards the priesthood. He and his colleagues, however, were almost as passionate in their nationalism as in their Catholicism and were reluctant to let the Vatican interfere with their racially exploitative colonial policies. Not until 1940, after the rise of European fascism, did Salazar hammer out a concordat with the Pope. He also signed a missionary accord in which the Vatican gave him control over the church in Angola. Thereafter Catholicism grew rapidly, and education, privilege and status, which could not be obtained through a state hide-bound by racism, could sometimes be sought through the church. In Huambo Protestants were partially eclipsed when catechists, seminarians, teachers, elders, wives, nuns, priests and swathes of other black Ovimbundu crowded into Catholic churches. Like earlier Protestant converts they adopted new names, new clothes, new furniture, new eating habits, and felt themselves to be superior to their kith and kin in spite of remaining 'native subjects' deprived of proper 'citizenship'.

Citizenship was the subject of a core piece of legislation, the Native Statute, introduced into Angola in 1926. The old class gradations of colonial society were legalistically replaced by the simple two-way barrier between 'citizens' and 'natives'. Natives were subject to a poll tax which replaced the old hut tax. Like natives in South Africa they were required to carry a pass-book which limited their movements and their employment opportunities. Those who made the grade as 'citizens', whether white, *mestizo*, or black, became legally entitled to set up businesses and could obtain loans from the Portuguese overseas bank. To be recognised as 'civilised' under the new ideology, an Angolan had to prove to a moral inspectorate that he or she was monogamous, spoke fluent Portuguese, ate with a knife and fork, and wore European clothes.

Anyone who did not meet these criteria, however loyal a member of the Catholic Church, and however distinguished his or her family history, was deemed to be a 'native'. And any native, as in the nineteenth century, was liable to be conscripted as a forced labourer. Under Salazar's New State, a 'non-civilised' subject, unlike a recognised citizen, suffered discrimination and remained painfully liable to pay the poll tax. The Native Statute of 1926 was later described as being not a ladder of opportunity but rather a gate which closed off many avenues of social or economic mobility.

The most socially complex part of Angola was Luanda, which remained distinctively different from anywhere else in the country—or indeed in Africa. The closest parallel might be found in the early Dutch settlements at the Cape of Good Hope. The literate community of Luanda city was very roughly divided into three social sections. The 'old *assimilados*', with roots going back to the seventeenth century, were primarily black Catholics. Pepetela's novel *A Gloriosa Familia* portrays the history of this almost aristocratic segment of society. A few of them may have acquired the odd white ancestor during the nineteenth century but mostly they remained fairly clannish. Aristocratic Luanda gentlemen married aristocratic Luanda brides. Their family trees can be traced through the records of army officers and school mistresses. 'Luso-Africans' of this class were sent out to govern the provinces and so slightly broadened their social horizons but their connection with the indigenous masses remained rather minimal. They spoke Portuguese at home, in their dance halls, at political meetings, and in upper-class bars. Like colonial settlers elsewhere in Africa, they used a kitchen vernacular, in their case Kimbundu, to speak to their servants. By the beginning of the twentieth century some members of the old aristocracy had felt that their status was being squeezed by the protagonists of rampant Victorian racism. In 1901 eleven high-status Creoles published a book of strident essays called *The Voice of Angola Crying out in the Wilderness*. They called themselves the 'true natives' of Angola to distinguish themselves from the black aborigines out in the sticks and from brown *mestizos* in the city. They complained bitterly about a loss of dignity and of status. They also protested that the law was making judgments which favoured white plaintiffs over black.

A second tranche of educated Luanda society consisted of 'new *assimilados*'. This group did not have deep urban traditions, like the old Creoles, but had acquired their veneer of urbanity through an education which became available from the late nineteenth century. They spoke enough Portuguese to seek jobs both in the public sector and in private enterprise, but Portuguese was not their mother tongue. At home they spoke Kimbundu and their family roots remained in the countryside. They established their own institutions and did not share those of the old black Catholics. Many new *assimilados* were not Catholics at all but the children of Protestant mission schools who worshipped in the Methodist chapels of the city. Their clubs and associations acquired discreet political aspirations that they sought to disguise from the surveillance of the police. The new *assimilados* were quite distinct from a third 'class' segment of upwardly-mobile Luanda residents, the *mestizo* element. A slowly rising tide of white carpet-baggers arriving in Luanda long remained predominantly male and, despite government disapproval, immigrant men often tied stable bonds with African women and cherished their mixed-race children. The experience of these *mestizo* children was very different from that of their counterparts in rural Angola who were often neglected and even despised. Luanda *mestizos* could sometimes aspire to an expatriate life-style with better economic resources than in any other African city. Some were even able to enter schools where they shared benches with white children.

The attitude of successive colonial regimes to the city *mestizos* was somewhat ambiguous. White politicians debated whether mixed-race children, a 'coloured' population in South African parlance, would enhance Angola's loyalty to Portugal or, by contrast, encourage an awakening of African nationalism. The problem of immigration and miscegenation was accentuated by a vexed question relating to the 2,000 white convicts living in Angola in the 1930s. The colonial minister, when visiting Angola, wrote to tell Salazar how shocked he was by the adverse effects of racial cohabitation. White convicts, he said, were living with black concubines and breeding a new generation which brought out the worst of the criminal element and the most base of the African one. Such intemperate racial views were seen as highly prejudicial by the mixed local populations but they also alienated potential immigrants who saw Angola as a 'convict colony' similar to Britain's old penal colony at Botany Bay. Criminal transportation to Luanda, where in the 1930s white convicts might still be seen wearing their prison chains, needed to be terminated. Portugal considered sending its criminals to the remote island of Timor in Indonesia. In the meantime migration to Angola stalled. The number of Portuguese leaving the colony, including a few repatriated convicts, rose to 3,500 a year and thus exceeded an in-coming migration of 3,000 a year. By the Second World War the attempt to transform Angola into a white settlement colony was far from complete.

6

COLONIALISM VERSUS NATIONALISM

In 1945 Salazar flew the flags at half-mast when he heard of the death of Hitler. The Portuguese colonies had gone through severe austerity during the Second World War but Portugal itself had made a few gains from its neutrality by trading tungsten to the German arms industry in exchange for gold bullion. In order—as a neutral country—to obtain essential supplies of wheat and petroleum from America the dictator had been required to lease a military air base on the Azores Islands to Britain and its allies. When the war was over Portugal was debarred from entering the United Nations and Salazar's colonies were not put into trusteeship as were those of Mussolini. Salazar's regime was authoritarian and racist but not really 'fascist', though it adopted some 'corporatist' policies from Italy. Poverty remained acute throughout the empire and in Europe only Albania was poorer than Portugal. Some British colonies, such as the Gold Coast, had by now achieved higher rates of literacy than Portugal itself. In Angola the colonial economy picked up slowly after the war and links to the mother-country improved with a makeshift air service which took five days to reach Lisbon. Shipping lines began once more to operate, bringing new white immigrants to Luanda. But above all Angola's post-war peasants and planters began to meet the world's deep craving for coffee. This brought a whole new dynamic to the economy of Angola.

The Angolan coffee industry had three different points of focus. The first and largest was in the old nineteenth-century coffee forests of the north, the second consisted of the Amboim plantations, and the third, more experimental, region was on a small corner of the Benguela highland where the climate was suitable for high-grade Arabica coffee rather than lowland Robusta coffee. High-grade coffee remained so scarce in Angola that when the directors of the Angolan coffee institute served their guests with coffee in porcelain cups on a silver salver they sourced it from Timor, at the furthest Asian end of the Portuguese empire. Quantity rather than quality was the basis of Angola's rise to near the top of the global league of coffee producers. Over the thirty years from the end of World War II in 1945 to independence in 1975 coffee production rose to 200,000 tons a year. Much of it was bought by the Dutch with their long-standing trade links to Angola. Dutch wax-print cloth in bright colours was particularly popular in Africa and was often emblazoned with images of national heroes. When the Dutch tried to sell cloth bearing pictures of Salazar, however, they had rapidly to desist, since—according to one famous Amsterdam dealer—'women were apt to display the dictator's face on inappropriate parts of their anatomy'.

In northern Angola some coffee was still grown after the world war on small plots owned by black peasants. It was possible to shell and dry coffee beans on a household scale rather than on an industrial scale. The trading and transporting of coffee, however, increasingly fell into the hands of white businessmen who bought the crop in exchange for essential household goods stocked in their village stores. This system gave the whip hand to the immigrants since each time there was a credit crisis shop-keepers took over ownership of plots held as debt security and the once-proud peasants became day labourers. The white land-holdings gradually became plantations which spread ever further into the forested north. As they grew, no adequate supply of local labour was available and so the new breed of coffee planters began recruiting *Gastarbeiter* from the highland of south-central Angola. These Ovimbundu strangers were naturally much resented by Kongo northerners who had now lost their land and their economic independence. The compulsory labour recruits from the south were equally unhappy to be torn from their own savannah farms to work long hours on foreign plantations in an unfamiliar environment full of snakes and ghosts and wizards. This unhappy social mix was a powder keg which was to explode in March 1961.

There were social problems in southern Angola too. One of Africa's leading historians, Basil Davidson, travelled across the region in 1954, opening the eyes of the world to the experiences of both the colonised and the colonisers. Among the colonisers he found that even a white engine driver in Angola earned less than a black one in Congo. The railway manager, on the other hand, thought Angola to be a 'little corner of paradise'. Among the colonised,

2,000 of the 15,000 railway employees were, in Davidson's words, 'slaves', compulsory labour recruits. The archives showed that 300,000 Angolans still lived under conditions of near slavery with minimal medical services and with wages of a few pence a day withheld until each labour contract had been satisfactorily completed. In 1954 a village chief who failed to supply a commissioner with the required number of conscripts was no longer given a shameful public flogging but he was bribed to meet a district quota laid down by the office of the governor-general. Labour was recruited not only formally for government projects such as road building, but also informally for private plantations which were each allocated about a dozen conscripts per planted acre of sugar cane or sisal fibres. A labour report of 1947 written by Henrique Galvão said that forced labour was used in Angola because of the continuing large-scale flight of workers to other colonies. The lack of social and medical services in Angola was reported to mean that infant mortality had reached 60 per cent. Privately-owned slaves, Galvão said, had to be kept as healthy as equally expensive horses, but there was no incentive to nurture government-supplied recruits in the same way. This report was soon suppressed and its author was thrown into gaol. Davidson noted that even in the towns few children were able to attend school and that by the age of ten they were liable to be arrested for 'vagrancy' and sent off to compulsory work-stations. He was so shocked by all that he saw and learnt that he remained a friend of Angola for the rest of his long life. He used his former skills as an intelligence officer among anti-Nazi guerrillas in the Balkans to gain an understanding of anti-colonial guerrillas in the Portuguese empire.

The key feature of the south remained the Benguela railway. Copper from southern Congo was a strategic world resource as it flowed across the highland to Lobito. The deep-water harbour had been built next to the railway on an ocean inlet during the 1920s. The trains carried cobalt as well as copper when mining prospered, particularly during the Korean War of the early 1950s. The up-trains also carried food supplies into Congo to feed the miners, dried fish from the barren coast and maize from the fertile highland. The old Scottish steam engines were still powered by wooden logs of blue gum and the company planted and harvested great swathes of Australian-type forest along the route. Thousands of Ovimbundu stokers fed the boilers and shovelled out the ash. Although these men enjoyed regular employment their rates of pay were minimal. Beyond the railway towns the government tried once more to establish white farming communities but, as ever, these could not be self-sustaining and required government compulsion to recruit black labour. Restiveness grew as the bush telegraph conveyed news of opportunities in Johannesburg where, it was believed, the streets were paved with gold. The Portuguese came to fear that exploiting peasant farmers for labour, be it locally, or by taking them to the desert fisheries, or by contracting them out to forest coffee estates, might cause an outburst of violent despair. Farmers were cautious people, however, and although their lives were hard they remained reluctant to listen to the siren calls that might bring forth a revolution.

In north-central Angola, on the dry and sparsely-peopled savannah lands beyond Ambaca, the colonial government thought that it could adopt policies previously tried by Germans in East Africa and Belgians in Congo. Instead of buying expensive cotton from America, the Portuguese would feed their domestic textile industry with home-grown cotton from the colonies. In each colonial case, however, the consequences of cotton policy were catastrophic: the Maji Maji rebellion shook German East Africa, harsh repression was applied in the Belgian Congo, and a blaze of revolution broke out in Angola. Cotton growing was a risky enterprise. The plant was introduced into areas where fertility was too low to grow commercial food crops but the cotton harvest could fail entirely in the event of drought or a plague of locusts. The risks were so high, and the rewards so low, that few white farmers were interested in venturing into cotton as some had thought to do at the time of the American civil war. Portugal's government decided to compel its Angolan subjects, Kimbundu people in the deep hinterland of Luanda, to grow cotton even if the consequences were regular spasms of starvation. Alarm bells were sounded as early as 1945 when a district commissioner reported that the cotton policy was leading to famine. His report reached the desk of the dictator in Lisbon. 'Famine', Salazar proclaimed archly, 'is a figment of the Bantu imagination'. He ordered his colonial minister, Marcello Caetano, to pursue the cotton policy with vigour and to drive 'lazy' Africans to work ever harder. The next dramatic spasm of famine occurred in January 1961 when desperate peasants burnt down the warehouses storing cotton seed for the new season's crop. They then picked up their emaciated children and fled across a river into the forest of the Congo Republic. As news of the uprising spread, Salazar sent planes to bomb the cotton villages. In the same month one of his political opponents decided to mount an ambitious public-relations coup. Henrique Galvão, the labour inspector now released from gaol, knew full well the real pain which colonial exploitation was imposing on Angola's farming communities. He therefore decided to hijack a cruise liner, the *Santa Maria*, and sail it to Luanda to awaken the world to the horrors that were being perpetrated in the name of civilisation.

The *Santa Maria* never did reach Angola but international journalists were excited by the adventure and hurried to Luanda to welcome a heroic Portuguese rebel. By happenstance these reporters were on hand when a quite different revolution broke out in the city streets on 4 February 1961. The February uprising, which culminated in Angola's independence fourteen years later, has a complex history and contested roots. Several incipient political pressure groups of exiles claimed to have planned the outbreak of violence. Portugal was willing to believe that revolutionary opposition was being coordinated and orchestrated. It is more likely, however, that the protest and the ensuing massacre were spontaneously sparked off by young local hotheads. These youths decided that they would attack the city gaol in an attempt to release some of their friends who had been rounded up by the secret police as potential trouble-makers. Their mini-coup failed but sent a shudder of panic through the white city. The winds of change, about which Britain's prime minister, Harold Macmillan, had recently made a famous speech, were sweeping through Africa. Settlers and expatriates were being widely replaced by black bourgeois entrepreneurs and bureaucrats as well as by politicians with neo-colonial supporters in Britain and France. The new nationalist governments elsewhere in Africa retained the old commercial, banking, insurance and transport links with former mother countries and continued to supply raw materials in exchange for manufactured consumer goods. Such a deal was not obviously open to Portugal in 1961 since the country still had a rather narrow industrial base. Colonists who had become accustomed to their racial privileges saw little advantage in returning to Europe and therefore took up spontaneous weapons to defend their status in Luanda. They set about attacking any educated black person who might aspire to become part of a middle class capable of administering the country, taking over white jobs and sending colonists back home to Europe. The government in Portugal approved the settler aspiration to defend privilege and, alarmingly, decided to issue gangs of vigilantes with real arms and ammunition. The ensuing massacre left a lasting legacy.

A few weeks after the Luanda uprising of February 1961, the northern explosion of March 1961 shook the colony even more violently. A dip in the market for coffee had meant that labourers were not being paid on time and so they politely marched up to a plantation office to ask for their arrears of wages. Their demonstration caused white panic. Settlers, having heard greatly exaggerated reports about racist confrontations across the frontier in Congo, assumed they were about to be attacked. As fear rippled through the north, settlers may have remembered the South African massacre at Sharpeville.

White gunfire broke out. Black counter-attacks were orchestrated across the region, some of them co-ordinated by an exiled political organisation across the border in Congo. Several hundred members of white families were killed, ten times more than all the Europeans who had been killed in the Mau Mau uprising in Kenya. Several thousand black people were killed too, some of them compulsory Ovimbundu migrants who had been deeply resented by the population of the north. The colonial administration took action and issued weapons to white vigilantes. On one English mission station the pastor, Archibald Patterson, was given twenty-four hours to leave the country. The next day all his teachers and catechists were killed and were buried under the school football pitch. Portugal cried 'wolf, wolf, the communists are coming'. America's new president, John F. Kennedy, was at first reluctant to come to the rescue having assumed that 'Africa for the Africans' would open doors to United States investment and opportunity. Salazar quietly told Kennedy that if the president did not help a staunch anti-communist ally such as Portugal his government would feel compelled to close America's mid-Atlantic air-base on the Azores Islands. American policy did a sharp U-turn and President Kennedy supplied Salazar's air-force with napalm to bomb rebellious forest villages. Thousands of Angolans fled across the northern frontier to the lower Congo where fellow countrymen, fellow members of the Baptist Church, welcomed them for a fourteen-year exile. In Kinshasa many petty bourgeois fishmongers, butchers, tailors and motor mechanics were white Portuguese from Lisbon who readily hired black Portuguese-speakers from Angola as helpmeets. Meanwhile the Angolan homeland underwent a generation of guerrilla warfare and of colonial counter-insurgency.

In 1961 Portugal feared that Angola's colonial days might be numbered. A radical change in imperial policy was therefore adopted by the dictatorship. A huge conscript army was built in the mother country and sent out to Africa, first to Angola but later also to Guinea and Mozambique. Army officers, who had put Salazar in power on condition that they should be purely ornamental, with smart uniforms and polished brass buttons, rather than an active force at risk of being called to arms, were so doubtful about the virtues of sending an expeditionary force to Africa that there were some attempts at mutiny. Soon the army's capacity for war was deeply challenged, not in Africa but in Asia where India conquered the Portuguese colony of Goa in 1961. Senior army commanders eventually realised, however, that a colonial war in Africa might be financially profitable. Informal trading deals developed and some members of the army gained control of a black market in currency. The Angolan war was nicknamed 'the war of the multi-stories' as each corrupt army officer used each of his furloughs to build a block of rental flats in Lisbon. Such high-level corruption was one of the legacies of colonialism in many parts of Africa. For the foot-soldiers the war was a much less happy experience. Death rates were high from road accidents, diseases, and even from fighting. Young men in Portugal began to migrate clandestinely to France, preferring to work in car factories rather than risk being conscripted for four years' dangerous and ill-paid service in Angola. The number of Portuguese in Paris soon far exceeded the number who served in Angola. To make good the shortfall in metropolitan conscripts, the colonial army, like other colonial armies, recruited black subjects as troops trained to target their own kith and kin. One of the most dangerous tasks facing the army was patrolling any dirt road into which nationalist guerrillas had planted anti-personnel mines. To avoid losing white soldiers and expensive equipment, black recruits were ordered to walk the sandy routes and so suicidally detonate the mines before the real army moved forward. In the longer term, strategic roads were tarred to make troop deployments faster and to hinder the planting of mines. Within a few years war had reached a virtual stalemate in the heartlands of Angola.

Salazar's second war strategy was economic. His nationalism had never been wholly successful in limiting foreign participation in Angola's economic development. The railways had been built by the British, the diamond mines were controlled by South Africa, the cotton agencies were financed by Belgium, and the Dutch sold textiles for coffee. When in 1963 the cost of defence required a dynamic search for new wealth which could be taxed, a policy of industrialisation was encouraged. The brewing of beer had been one of the first import substitution industries in African colonies and in Angola brewing became so successful that it not only supplied local markets but also met the thirsty demand of western Congo where colonial industries were collapsing. Enterprises producing textiles, furniture, house-paint, dry foods, cigarettes and building materials all proliferated. A relaxation on foreign investments allowed European and American management methods, technologies and patents to enter the country. The big investment, however, was in petroleum, though Salazar mourned the opening of the first oil wells. He said that they would bring an end to his dream of a land fit for poor, happy, peasants who needed little by way of manufactured consumer goods and did not hanker after expensive government services in education, or health, or housing. The great dictator apparently believed, quite genuinely, that he was doing the best for his peasants and was therefore deeply mortified when in

1963 Charles Boxer, the grand master of Portuguese imperial history, published a devastating book, *Race Relations in the Portuguese Colonial Empire*, which demolished some of Portugal's patriotic myths about its colonial achievements.

When oil wells were opened in Cabinda the royalties which flowed from Texas did enable Salazar, despite his reservations, to finance his army. Military success was further ensured with subsidised war materials from South Africa which was anxious to hinder the spread of African nationalism down to the border of Namibia. The United States also continued to help the dictatorship by illegitimately allowing Portugal to use NATO weapons officially designed to protect the north Atlantic from communism. These were now deployed to defend the Portuguese colonies against the alleged threat of communism in Africa.

The insurgents, seeking the freedom which Salazar so feared and detested, came from a variety of regional backgrounds and had different ideologies. When the war for independence broke out in 1961 the first group which tried to ride the tiger of anti-colonial rebellion was a union of northern peoples with a variety of safe havens in Congo where Belgians had allowed the proliferation of ethno-cultural associations. Various factions eventually came together as the Front for the National Liberation of Angola, FNLA. Angola's northern political union was able to gain international sponsorship and even set up a provisional government-in-exile modelled on the exiled government of Algeria. In addition to recognition by several newly-independent African governments, and by a Pan-African committee devoted to the furthering of decolonisation, the so-called 'national' front of the north managed to get support from both China and America. It was not, however, favoured by the Soviet Union. A different liberation movement, which did enjoy Soviet backing, arose in Luanda and its hinterland. This Movement for the Popular Liberation of Angola, the MPLA, was loosely the heir to the clubs, associations and newspapers which successive colonial regimes has suppressed. It tried to establish its exiled leadership in Congo-Léopoldville but was soon driven out by its rival and took refuge in Congo-Brazzaville, on the opposite bank of the river. There it had no frontier with mainland Angola but only with the famous enclave of Cabinda, on the coast north of the Congo River. It was there that the movement set up a small guerrilla army. Pepetela, a white activist in the campaign for Angolan liberation, portrayed the army's every-day life in his novel *Mayombe*. Fear and boredom, he said, were the twin hallmarks of guerrilla warfare. The young volunteers in forest camps in 'ex-French' Congo constantly longed for better food or a cigarette and then suddenly they were hurled into a cross-border raid from which many did not return. Their political masters, meanwhile, moved some of the senior staff far away to the safe city of Dar-es-Salaam, cheek by jowl with exiled leaders from Mozambique and South Africa, and received support from the government of Tanzania.

The leader of the MPLA was Agostinho Neto, a typical product of Angola's complex cultural history. He came from the Kimbundu hinterland of Luanda but spoke excellent Portuguese and used it to write poetry. Although a black African, he associated freely with city Creoles and *mestizos*. His father had been a Methodist minister who gave his son such a good western education that he won a scholarship to study medicine in Lisbon. Like several other African statesmen, Neto married a white woman which caused some purists to be suspicious of his commitment to the black cause. He was surreptitiously active in student circles in Portugal, and even more surreptitiously established links with the outlawed communist party in Lisbon. He served at least one term in a Portuguese prison when the secret police feared his subversive influence. When Amnesty International was founded, it chose Neto as its first prisoner of conscience and when he escaped from Portugal he arrived at the London office, a bemused and bespectacled poet. He thereafter unexpectedly grew to become a guerrilla commander and the treasurer of the popular liberation movement. It was Neto who gained the resources to be able to hand out carrots, wield sticks, orchestrate policy, and promote guerrilla officers. He set up his bush camps in Zambia and supplied them as best he could with weapons hauled up the 1,000-mile dirt road from Dar-es-Salaam. On one of his forays across the border into Angolan territory he took Basil Davidson with him. Davidson's classic book, *In the Eye of the Storm*, revealed the aspirations of the liberation movement to its worldwide sympathisers.

The south of Angola had a different political trajectory from the north and the centre of the country. A few southern exiles joined the northern FNLA bandwagon in Kinshasa, providing some of the military and political leadership. Soon, however, they felt despised and instead of their haughty Ovimbundu pedigrees being recognised they were marginalised like country bumpkins. By 1964 the southerners had virtually broken their ties with the élitist Kongo and within two years had created a liberation movement of their own, UNITA, the Union for the Independence of the Totality of Angola. They eventually gained an exile base in newly-independent Zambia. Their leader, an ambitious young man of boundless confidence, used every possible network to create a united southern political movement. His association with the churches, which had been installed on the highland by Swiss and American missionaries, enabled him to use old-boy networks from the Protestant schools to mobilise some support. He also had good contacts with the Benguela railway on which his father had been employed, and a group of people linked to each other through service on the railway was able to use its telegraph to maintain subversive communications. Last but not least, Jonas Savimbi was one of the few Ovimbundu who did know his way around the diplomatic circuit. He had been a student in Portugal as well as in Switzerland, though his attempt to study medicine had proved abortive. Instead he had taken courses in politics at the University of Lausanne and called himself 'Doctor' in the way the honorific title was used in Portugal to denote any university graduate. As Dr Savimbi he moved to the United States to further his political ambition, but for all his personal drive and cosmopolitan experience, he was initially unable, on his return to Africa, to build either an effective political movement or a competent guerrilla army. By the early 1970s he had entered into secret negotiations with officers in the Portuguese army over the possibility of obtaining a neo-colonial settlement of the liberation stalemate. He naturally sought a powerful personal role for himself despite his as yet minimal grassroots support in the country.

Writing a history of the FNLA, MPLA, and UNITA represents a tough challenge. Guerrilla movements do not have the resources to store many archives, or even the paper and ink to write many records. Oral testimonies, on the other hand, had constantly to be modified to meet changing scenarios and, with hindsight, place the narrator in the best available light. When a *coup d'état* occurred in Lisbon in April 1974, however, it opened up an astonishing new source of information. The archives of the secret police were thrown wide open. This police force had been introduced into Angola in the late 1950s to monitor any subversive activity among settlers, some of whom had voted for a presidential candidate who proposed to dismiss Salazar. Some restless immigrants might even have aspired unilaterally to declare white independence in Angola. Once the liberation war had broken out, however, the main purpose of the political police was to monitor black subversion. As a consequence the police held a much better paper trail of changing rebel aspirations than did the liberation movements themselves. Scholars, exploring the newly-opened Lisbon range of civilian, diplomatic, economic and military archives, fell thankfully on the police harvest of ephemeral memoranda, handbills, speeches and committee minutes produced, but rarely saved, by rival liberation movements. Ironic though it may seem, the defeated colonising enemy preserved a better set of records than the victorious liberation movements. The documents frozen in police files had not undergone the process of adaptation which oral records underwent as each survivor tried to reinterpret his or her personal trajectory in the light of changing circumstances. The value of the police records has to be tempered with sensitive care, however, when dealing with interview materials. In Angola torture was used in dark cells to extract information from victims screaming with pain. The army also used terrorism openly when village leaders were publicly beheaded to dissuade colonial subjects from even thinking about independence. Terror and torture did not lead to reliable oral testimonies.

Many of the attempts to understand Angola's history in the second half of the twentieth century were undertaken by foreign scholars who were deeply sympathetic to Angola's protracted traumas but who came from another world, or wrote in another language. Their work often depended on diplomatic documents or on interviews with exiled leaders. Gradually, however, the voice of the voiceless began to be heard through interviews with ordinary survivors. In 1997 Drumond Jaime and Helder Barber published extensive interviews with the founding fathers—Angola has very few founding mothers—who had survived the vicissitudes of independence in their local communities. The oral record is naturally controversial as Christine Messiant, with humorous perspicacity, once pointed out to a large history congress which included war veterans assembled in Luanda's old Monumental Cinema. 'Here in Angola', she said, 'even the past is unpredictable'. One of the outstanding historians of the anti-colonial campaigns was a Brazilian scholar, Marcelo Bittencourt, author of two volumes on the subject, *Estamos Juntos*, 'we all stand shoulder-to-shoulder'. Bittencourt digested the work of the international scholars, expanded the range of interview materials, and made extended use of the new archives. His work enabled a rising student generation to get a better grasp of the factionalism which marked the kaleidoscope of Angola's political history. Bittencourt's convincing understanding of the interaction between daily life and liberation politics is partly based on interviews conducted in Luanda between 1995 and 2000. His timing was felicitous since some old men had survived the wars and were still able to respond to detailed questionnaires which sought to clarify, from various vantage points, the issues which newly discovered archival papers had raised. Political movements formed, splintered, and re-formed in cities of exile or in rudimentary forest camps. The very creation of the MPLA was subject to rival memories and interpretations. The study of factionalism in the Angolan liberation struggles had gone in cycles of academic fashion which at one moment emphasised ideology, at another ethnicity, at another foreign sponsorship, at another education and culture. Always the skills, ambitions, and weaknesses of individual militants, politicians, diplomats, entrepreneurs, played a role. So too did the minor irritants or comforts of life on the move, in exile, in rudimentary camps, in rented mud huts. And always race remained a part of the colonised mindset, an awareness so prevalent that foot-soldiers, perceiving little progress on the ground, wondered whether leaders with white spouses might not have made secret deals with the 'tribes' of their in-laws. Being even half white in Angola could lead to accusations of petty bourgeois snobbery and a suspicion of neglecting the welfare of the 2–3,000 men in the MPLA's various mini-regiments of guerrillas.

In Angola, the years before the fall of Portugal's dictatorship were those in which lassitude and disenchantment overcame optimism and ambition after ten years of ineffectual struggle. Blame and counter-blame, leadership bids and counter-bids, solidarity and fragmentation, class rivalry and ethnic fraternity, all of them affected both the FNLA and the MPLA, and even the still minuscule UNITA, with its 300 isolated militants covertly attempting to seek military alliances with disaffected Portuguese troops in the deepest east. Rumblings, accusations, arrests and executions accompanied the political evolution of each faction. A 'readjustment movement', which came from China, a distant and little-known force on the nationalist scene, attempted to bring clarity to MPLA ideology, and one of Angola's founding fathers, Viriato da Cruz, retired from active politics to settle in the People's Republic. The Chinese fashion for self-criticism took hold in the Angolan camps and created seminars attended by numbers of middle cadres and common foot-soldiers. They discussed the predicaments of exile, the successes and failings of the leadership, the injustices and inequalities which separated the 'civilised' nationalists from Angola's towns and the 'indigenous' guerrillas from the countryside. None of the leaders was comfortable with such grass-root criticism and Agostinho Neto was particularly bitter in his condemnation of dissidence. As the absolute ruler of his movement he controlled the money and rewarded the faithful while punishing those who were disloyal—a style of political management which survived into independent Angola. The last colonial years did not augur well for the creation of a vibrant new civil society with a climate of open debate.

The end of empire was brought nearer when António Salazar, Europe's most durable dictator, finally died in 1970 after ruling Portugal and its colonies with an iron fist for no fewer than forty years. When he was struck down by a stroke, power passed to Marcello Caetano, his former minister for colonial affairs. Although some hoped for change, they discovered that when Caetano appeared to signal left, he actually turned right and in the last five years of colonial rule, from 1969 to 1974, practice remained largely autocratic. One change of policy in the early 1970s did, however, concern Angola's all-important coffee industry. Instead of repression, as practised on the highland, the new imperial government decided to adopt a policy of conciliation towards the black élite of the north and allow its members a limited return to independent coffee growing and marketing, with transport in the hands of co-operatives managed by local members of the Baptist church. The initiative was much resented by white businessmen but it was seen by the Portuguese military as creating reliable allies, wedded to market principles, and therefore unlikely to be seduced by any virulent nationalistic aspirations advocated by Marxist or Maoist political exiles. A policy of winning hearts and minds, however, came too late, and Angola began to disintegrate.

By the early 1970s the MPLA was also beginning to fall apart, with violent rivalry breaking out along ethnic, ideological and class lines. Two rebellious factions split from the party. The 'eastern rebellion' took some of the leadership, along with militants and guerrillas who had been recruited in the highland, out of the camps in the eastern savannah and eventually into alliance with rival movements. The 'active rebellion' of some of the more intellectual members of the Angolan élite despaired of making any progress under the command of Agostinho Neto and adopted its own breakaway ideological agenda. The Soviet Union, weary of this factionalism among its erstwhile protégés, suspended accreditation and logistical support.

A new future for Angola suddenly and unexpectedly began on 25 April 1974 when the world turned upside down. Angola's politicians were as surprised as those of Portugal when the Lisbon government was overthrown without a shot being fired. The coup which felled Caetano and packed him off to exile in Brazil had little to do with either the FNLA or the MPLA but was mounted by young military captains in the Portuguese army. These junior officers had decided that they were not going to win lucrative benefits from the colonial war in the way their elders had done in the 1960s. Simultaneously Portugal's leading industrialists came to the realisation that their Lisbon enterprises would face a better future in democratic Europe than in colonial Africa. Business also resented the everlasting burden of war taxes. It was well-informed, though secretive, bankers who predicted the fall of the dictatorship while both Western and Eastern intelligence agencies, as well as Portugal's own security services, were completely oblivious to any change in the air.

The unexpected events in Lisbon led to a re-alignment of forces in Angola. Exiles began to arrive in Luanda and factions negotiated deals with their rivals. The Soviet Union reversed its decision to abandon Angola and hastily arranged for weapons to be supplied, advisers to be trained, and Cuban troops to be put on standby, for any vicarious intervention that might seem appropriate as the Portuguese prepared to leave Africa. In January 1975 an interim government was established. Its four-power executive included not only the old imperial power, Portugal, but also all three nationalist parties, FNLA, MPLA, and UNITA.

7

THE STRUGGLES OF THE SEVENTIES

The birth-pangs of the new independent nation of Angola were protracted and bloody, compounded by the presence of a multiplicity of midwives: Congolese, Russian, Cuban, South African and American. The colonial war had ended abruptly in April 1974 and by January 1975 the four-power executive was established. The colonial war and the colonial truce were soon followed, however, by a new war, the war of foreign intervention. Each of the three indigenous military movements wanted to establish its own supremacy and each called for support from neighbours and allies. Rivalry led to conflict and the first salvoes of a fratricidal war which led to the war of intervention were fired in July 1975. MPLA troops, summoned from guerrilla camps in the remote east and havens of exile abroad, converged on Luanda. In the ensuing week of violence the Luanda returnees were supported by irregular militias mobilised by the local party leadership which had been organising activist cells of 'people power' in the city. Their opponents were the rather smarter army of exiles which came down from the north. Within days the four-way power-sharing executive, established as an interim government, was disbanded. The armies and politicians of both the northern FNLA and the southern UNITA were driven out of the city, leaving the MPLA and the Portuguese in control.

The leaders of UNITA had to make a quick decision. Should they sue for peace, and form a political alliance with the MPLA, or should they re-join their uncomfortable former allies in the FNLA? Savimbi's initial inclination, as a one-time admirer of Mao Zedong, was to accept the advice of radical

Portuguese soldiers and join forces with the MPLA. He soon realised, however, that neither South Africa nor the United States was likely to tolerate the advent of a 'Maoist' or 'Marxist' regime in independent Angola. Savimbi therefore decided to look for an alternative alliance. He hoped that he and the other southern leader, Daniel Chipenda, might negotiate a deal with the FNLA which would give them significant military purchase and access to foreign support. Chipenda was apparently in contact with South Africa, a neighbour which later became a key supporter of Savimbi. By September 1975 the MPLA was being held at bay in much of the south and UNITA dominated the old kingdoms of Bihé and Huambo.

The MPLA offensive then had to turn to the north but the FNLA had gained the support of General Mobutu, the president of Congo. American policy, governed at the time by Henry Kissinger, in covert association with the secret services, put its faith in the FNLA to install a pro-Western regime in Luanda. The methods adopted were deeply flawed, however, and an incompetent band of multinational mercenaries was soon worsted, leaving the United States angry and embarrassed. Worse was to follow when it emerged that American oil executives had been keeping their own options open by paying petroleum royalties to an interim MPLA administration which the American government had been attempting to overthrow by violent means.

After the American discomfiture in the north, it was in the south that a more dramatic foreign intervention occurred. South Africa sent advisors to counsel UNITA on ways of outwitting the MPLA. Later the South Africans supplied combat troops as well, although they took care to mask their identity and avoid a world outcry at the sight of Afrikaner soldiers appearing to spread *apartheid*. At the same time the MPLA equally discreetly received a first contingent of 500 Cuban military instructors to help stiffen resistance against the resurgent south. Military instructors from the Caribbean proved quite insufficient, however, to stop what became a full-scale South African invasion when a 'Zulu Column' of armoured vehicles was sent up the Angolan coast road and captured the port of Lobito. In retaliation for the South African invasion Cuban commandos were sent down the road between Luanda and Lobito to prevent further lightning South African progress along the seashore. A second South African column, code-named Foxbat, took an inland route and drove much deeper into Angola. It only halted when it reached the northern edge of the highland, poised to advance on Luanda, but it was cautious lest it meet Cuban troops head-on.

The night of 10 November 1975 was an eventful one in the city of Luanda. In years to come Angolans keen to share the camaraderie of momentous memory would ask each other 'Where were you on the November night in 1975?' It had long been agreed that Portugal would grant independence to Angola the following day. As the MPLA prepared to celebrate the arrival of freedom, excited but apprehensive citizens could hear Congolese guns pounding the northern city suburbs in support of the FNLA. Meanwhile, to the south, Cuban guns, partly staffed by the militants of the MPLA, held at bay the *Blitzkrieg* columns of South Africa's expeditionary force. Off-shore, Portugal's last governor-general sailed away declaring that 'sovereignty' had been transferred to 'the people of Angola'.

The battle for Luanda is documented by several different sources which dovetail in an unusually satisfying manner. Marina Rey Cabrera edited accounts of the Cuban participation in the Angolan wars, complete with battle plans and diagrams written by senior officers in the Cuban expeditionary army. John Stockwell published a first-hand history of the American involvement in the war of intervention, giving details of the type and quantity of weapons that he had supplied to the Central Intelligence Agency's prospective client armies. Ryszard Kapuscinski wrote a vivid description of the battle fronts, and also of their wider context, for his Polish news agency as he hitch-hiked his way around the country, by road and by air, in the last days before independence. Franz-Wilhelm Heimer analysed the political significance of the events, and Christine Messiant wrote a thesis on the sociological background to the competing factions in Angola's militarised society.

As so often, fiction provides an insight into the variety of expectations among those caught up in the war. The old Benguela trader, Alexander Semedo, the hero of Pepetela's novel, *Yaka*, had both white and *mestizo* grandchildren whom he greatly cherished as he watched them playing football. When the crisis of intervention broke some white members of his family sought to find a racial haven in South Africa. Others, equally white, became wildly excited by the radical new ideas of nationalism and therefore supported the MPLA. The rest of the family, by contrast, kept their heads down and tried to persuade their grandfather to emigrate to Portugal, the land of his forefathers. Alexander, however, had been born a white Angolan and trusted in the protection of the family fetish, the Yaka with the amber eyes, who had guarded his loved ones through all the upheavals of the twentieth century. He lived on in Pepetela's fictional world.

The MPLA enjoyed the support not only of some of Pepetela's fictional characters but also of a great many Angolan citizens, some of whom flocked to join its volunteer army. Others, however, both north and south, opposed the party's dominance in Luanda and, helped by 6,000 South African troops, established an alternative highland capital in Huambo, unofficially known as the headquarters of the 'Democratic' Republic of Angola. After celebrating independence day on 11 November 1975, the MPLA attacked its rivals. Within weeks the Cuban soldiers who had been flown in during the last days of colonial rule were reinforced by a seaborne expeditionary army which outnumbered the South African invading force. This Cuban contingent soon rose to 10,000 men equipped with heavy long-range guns and armoured personnel carriers. The MPLA recovery of the provinces began with an attack on the north where the United States covertly but ineffectually tried to maintain its support for the FNLA with its borrowed regiments from the Congo army. This American backing could be neither extensive nor public since, in the months following the loss of Vietnam in April 1975, the US Congress was reluctant to approve any new foreign adventures. The Washington government had been compelled to use stealth in building up armed clients capable of supporting its preferred political options in Angola. A dozen small rented planes flew consignments of weapons to the raw recruits of both the FNLA and UNITA but attempts to stiffen United States' allies proved to be another humiliating fiasco which further tarnished Washington's post-Vietnam reputation.

Worse was to follow when news of the South African invasion of Angola became a global news story. Such was the profound horror with which the West viewed the racial policies which South Africa practised at home that attitudes towards Angola, and to the war of intervention, changed throughout Africa and beyond. Sympathy for the Huambo 'democratic' regime rapidly dwindled and toleration of the Luanda 'popular' government grew even among members of the Organisation of African Unity who were traditionally suspicious of Soviet adventurism in Africa. By January 1976 the MPLA forces had effectively recovered the north and were strong enough to attack the south. The alliance between FNLA and UNITA began to unravel in factional disputes. The South African expeditionary army, dismayed at the military incompetence, the administrative waywardness, and the black racism of its UNITA allies, decided to cut its losses. As South Africa drew back into Namibia, both UNITA and the FNLA collapsed. The MPLA took over the whole of the country. Only roving bands of dissidents continued to operate in remote districts of the south-east. US intelligence estimated that its covert contribution of $30 million to the arming of the FNLA and UNITA had been dwarfed by a Russian grant of $400 million, spent on arming the MPLA and its Cuban allies. The South Africans had spent $130 million on their cross-border campaign by March 1976 when they pulled out in a glare of unwelcome publicity. But the biggest loser had been Congo whose large and well-funded army had proved to be a paper tiger.

No sooner had the war of intervention ended than the new Luanda government had to put all its scarce political skills and energies into building the future. The MPLA inherited colonial legacies which were deeply entrenched and Angolan society was found to be as complex as any in Africa. Creating a viable civil society for the nation as a whole would be difficult. Some old Creoles, whose status had dwindled in the later colonial years, and who had discreetly associated with the 1960 nucleus of the MPLA, saw their stock rise again. Other future leaders gained their academic qualifications and world experience in exile in France or Germany or in newly independent African nations like ex-French Guinea. Some made subversive contact with radical politicians in the underground opposition to Salazar's dictatorship. Bringing Angolan radicals together to form an effective ruling party which bridged the differences between a black class of new *assimilados* and the competitive sons and daughters of white settlers with black marriage partners who could give them status, sponsor their education, or find them suitable employment in business or in the civil service, was a challenge. As it grew, the MPLA had also attracted radical white members and some members of the historical class of old Creoles. After independence, the colonial niceties of race, pedigree, language, education, and ambition were to haunt the MPLA as it struggled to create a stable ruling establishment in the capital city. Despite their differences all of the assimilated factions of urban society, new and old, black and brown, had a significant advantage in terms of opportunity when compared to the throngs of job-seekers who flocked to the city from the largely illiterate hinterland. The educated minority also had a political edge over the people of the far interior—whether in the south or the north—when it came to bargaining over the future of Angola. Language was power in postcolonial African politics and it was the assimilated class which spoke Portuguese, the language of command.

Once the MPLA had secured its hold on the country, disputes within the ruling circle over the nature of the new nation were many. Was Angola to be a radical country with an ideology of egalitarianism which broke with the traditions of class, race and privilege that had been so prominent in the colonial period? Or had the struggle for survival been so disruptive of the élite's way of life that continuity needed to be tightly clasped and old institutions tenaciously maintained? The party also asked itself whether the new leadership was to be the one which had spoken to the world from exile in Dar-es-Salaam, or was power to be placed in the hands of those Angolans who had lived in Luanda during the long night of the colonial occupation? Was authority to be exercised by political theorists or pragmatic administrators, and would power go to the civilian committee men or to the military who held the guns? Equally controversial was the question of whether the senior military men would be those who had fought the colonial forces to a standstill on the remote savannah frontier or the proud pioneers who had maintained the flag of liberation in a rural fastness outside the city of Luanda. Rarely had the political heirs in any African colony been more faction-ridden than those who took up the reins of power in Angola. The responsibilities facing the inexperienced cadres who constituted the new government were awesome.

The MPLA soon discovered that coming to terms with the management of a city, a bureaucracy, an economy and a country was a greater challenge than driving out their regional enemies with the help of a disciplined Cuban military force. In the long term it was political, economic and administrative mismanagement which brought systematic instability to postcolonial Angola. Although nearly half of the Cubans in the country were civilians deployed in rebuilding the infrastructure, the city and the country were nonetheless profoundly disrupted by the flight of 90 per cent of white public-service personnel. Disorder regularly opened up opportunities for rivals to seek power, and brought a return of interventionist foreign armies both from the Congo north and from the South African south.

The mismanagement of government was caused both by inexperience and by fatal rifts in the ideological positions of the members of the ruling party. Most colonial heirs, particularly in Francophone Africa but to a lesser extent also in Anglophone Africa, inherited an entrenched legal framework, a functioning civil service, an internationally recognised currency and an integrated army. In Angola the abrupt departure of most of Portugal's soldiers, bankers, administrators and lawyers left few functioning institutions which could be adapted to the new political circumstances. But the failure of the MPLA to pick up the colonial mantle and create a recognisably normal postcolonial, or neo-colonial, state was not exclusively due to a shortage of experienced personnel. Difficulties were compounded by a resurgent military insecurity in the all-important oil province of Cabinda. A separatist movement aspired to gain independence for the enclave, which was cut off from the Angolan mainland by the Congo River and by a finger of Congo territory. The rulers of Congo would naturally have liked to annex this once-Portuguese territory which had become the source of most of Angola's petroleum. Congo gave discreet support to any troublemakers whom it could sponsor and the military insecurity in Cabinda had far-reaching consequences. Instead of reducing the size of the Cuban expeditionary force after the South Africans had withdrawn, the MPLA was obliged to maintain, and pay for, a continued Cuban presence strong enough to protect the Cabinda oil installations. These oil wells were operated by the Texan firm Gulf Oil and, paradoxically, it was out of oil royalties that Cuban military salaries were paid. Since the United States was at odds with Cuba over its revolutionary propaganda in the Caribbean and Latin America, and also with Angola over its friendship with the Soviet Union, Washington was somewhat dismayed that Texas was sponsoring 'Moscow's Ghurkhas' to protect its oil assets in Africa. Rather more serious than Washington's coolness was the fact that insecurity in Cabinda prevented the Angolan government from concentrating on the building of a stable political system and on repairing the damage done to the national economy by the interventionist war.

While security in the oil fields was distracting the government from the task of national reconstruction, another irritating legacy of the interventionist war began to fester in the south. The leader of UNITA, Jonas Savimbi, built up racial tension by accusing the Luanda regime of being in the pocket of foreigners. He alleged that the MPLA government was not only staffed by whites but was excessively parochial in its ethnic preference for Kimbundu citizens. Savimbi's xenophobic, racist and ethnic rhetoric culminated in a strident proposal for the creation of a 'black republic' of Angola to replace the one which allegedly favoured old Creoles, *assimilados*, *mestizos*, and white immigrants. By playing the race card, and thereby opening a whole box of repressed colonial neuroses, the UNITA leader was lighting the fuse of a powder trail which had long and painful consequences for any postcolonial reconciliation and reconstruction. Savimbi, who had once been sponsored by China, also tried momentarily to play the 'socialist' card. He gambled that this was a direction which Africa would favour and so he tried to prove that the MPLA were not the 'true' socialists of Angola. These strategies did not succeed, however, since the race theme did not play well with potential UNITA supporters in Washington or Lisbon and the socialist one did not gain UNITA any credit with Pretoria or Kinshasa. Savimbi had to modify his stance on both scores in his search for international backing. In the meantime, however, the MPLA once more had to postpone the demobilisation of its army in order to keep a wary eye on the disaffected south where Savimbi's voice was heard most clearly.

While the Luanda government was putting scarce political and military energies into resolving issues of intervention and regional security, it was seriously neglecting its own constituency in the city where it expected its core support to be solid. Thus it was that while the infant government was distracted by distant horizons, it suddenly found that the ground had been dramatically cut from under its feet in its own urban backyard. In May 1977 an attempted *coup d'état* came perilously close to overthrowing the government of Agostinho Neto and resulted in the death of several senior members of his cabinet. In the city, the expectation that independence would bring rich rewards to young black people had led to constant disappointment through no less than two years of austerity. Suddenly the frustration of those who had won little from independence, and who were intensely jealous of the cosmopolitan élite which had inherited the colonial trappings of power and the visible symbols of prosperity, exploded in violent despair.

The political thinker behind the attempted coup was Nito Alves, a black military leader from the Luanda backlands. Although he was subsequently accused of being a racist who had incited the black masses of the slums to rise up against the lighter-skinned cadres in the popular movement, he was in fact more concerned with high-minded ideals than with race-based jealousies. He gained some of these political ideas from his female ideological sparring partner, Sita Valles, a radical whose father had come to Angola from Portuguese India and who was familiar with Marxist forms of discourse. Nito Alves' authority stemmed largely from having been a self-reliant military commander who had held out in forest hide-outs for more than a decade. His men attacked military patrols, ambushed convoys on the roads from the city to the north, and threatened the heavily-fenced plantation houses on the coffee-estates. His guerrilla heroism, his radical turn of phrase, and his initial support for Agostinho Neto, won him the right to political office. They did not, however, make him a member of the inner circle of cosmopolitan leaders who had spent the liberation wars travelling in exile and who expected to be the unchallenged masters of the country on their return.

As the fruits of freedom eluded the populace, the marginalised militants turned from the politics of compromise to the mobilisation of ordinary people. In the poor quarters of Luanda Nito Alves organised study groups in which to debate the ideal of independence, the belief in equality, and the strategy for finding employment after the departure of the 200,000 whites who had fled the country in 1975. At first Agostinho Neto and his party leaders had applauded the mobilisation of street power among 'their people'.

'Peasants' and 'workers' had always been the heroes of the MPLA's armed struggle although the peasant credentials of the leadership were conspicuously thin and their understanding of the aspirations of workers was quite naïve. Once the foreign invaders had been driven out in 1976, the MPLA relaxed and failed to perceive the danger signals emanating from the townships on its doorstep. While members of the central committee shared out the spoils of affluence, helping themselves to the villas and sailing yachts left behind by the fleeing white community, people in the street were having difficulty finding enough to eat.

As power and wealth corrupted the victors, the poor began to realise that their own aspirations required a different agenda. Out in Sambizanga, on the edge of the asphalt city, it was the local football club that became the venue for illicit political debate. Football had been the circus which Salazar, like Mussolini before him, had offered his people to quench their otherwise dangerous political thirst, and football was accepted by the new nationalists as an appropriate focus for patriotism. In Sambizanga, however, the passion for the sport did not obliterate the desire for social justice or assuage the anger of the people when an incompetent regime was unable to make good a lack of food. So serious did shortages become that the government sent troops into the slums to search out 'hoarders' who could be blamed for withholding stocks of flour from 'the people'. Incensed football fans met to plot subversion.

When the revolution of 27 May 1977 broke, inspired by Nito Alves' study groups, the attack on the government was actually orchestrated by a faction of the army led by José van Dunem, a member of one of the most distinguished of the Creole families. The military rebel had spent the last years of the colonial war in a concentration camp in the southern desert. On release his associates, known as the 'prison graduates', kept their ears close to the ground. After two years of austerity and disappointment the rebels confidently expected to receive mass support from the city slums should they attempt to replace Neto's ministers with new leaders. The radicals who launched the uprising against the old MPLA stalwarts also assumed that their populist credentials would win them approval from the Soviet Union. When the crunch came, however, the Soviets were slow to decide whether to support Agostinho Neto, the elderly leader, or Nito Alves, the vigorous young ideologue. It was the Cubans who made the decision to back the old guard rather than support the younger generation. Cuban troops moved with alacrity, seized the Luanda radio station, broadcast the news—in Spanish—that the putsch had failed, and briskly set about making sure that Agostinho Neto and his surviving cabinet colleagues retained power. Coup leaders were caught and indiscriminately killed. Their radical sympathisers were terrified into submission.

The reprisals which the rattled government subsequently took against anyone who might have been involved in the uprising were so savage that Angola was set on a downward path of spiralling violence outstripping the cruelties of the colonial war and the brutalities of the war of intervention. From 1977 fear stalked the land and guns outweighed ideals in determining the path to the future. Far from disbanding the much-hated secret police, a Portuguese legacy initially built on a Gestapo model, the coup survivors used political security forces to repress any independence of thought that might inflame the aspirations of the urban population. The blood-stained crisis of May 1977 led to fundamental changes in the country's management. From aspiring to be a mass movement, seeking support throughout the city, the ruling MPLA turned itself into a self-selected élite party mendaciously calling itself 'the vanguard of the workers'.

At the same time that the government was adopting its new dictatorial mode at home, it was also bringing to a conclusion the 1970s phase of the wars of intervention on the frontiers. The ending of the war between Angola and Congo was made possible in 1978 by the resolution of an acrimonious Belgian colonial legacy which had long affected the security of both countries. Angola discovered that it could hold Congo to ransom through the presence on its side of the border of rebel troops from the wealthy copper province of Katanga in southern Congo. These troops, known as the Katanga *gendarmerie*, had been refugees in Portuguese Angola ever since they had been driven from their homeland by a United Nations multinational army following a failed secessionist rebellion in 1963. The *gendarmes* had allegedly been used by the Portuguese to hunt down nationalist guerrillas in the colonial war but when Portugal was defeated they formed an alliance with the MPLA. Their ambition was to seek a way of returning to Congo and recapturing political power in their old province of Katanga. Angola was delighted at the prospect that these exiles might be able to weaken the Congo government of Mobutu, which had done so much to hinder a peaceful transition to independence in Angola. A first attack on Katanga by the *gendarmerie* was launched in 1977 and caused the Congo army to crumble when some of the local population of the copper province welcomed the invaders as liberators. Western investors in the copper mines were appalled, however, at the concept of 'liberation' from the safe rule of their chosen dictator, General Mobutu. France hastily recruited a client army in Morocco and flew it to Katanga to drive out the cross-border invaders. Such neo-colonial interference was only a temporary deterrent, however, and in 1978 the *gendarmerie* invaded again. Once more Mobutu's defence forces were worsted. This time the United States intervened and flew in an even heavier assortment of regiments borrowed from regimes sympathetic to the West. The copper mines were rescued, again.

After facing two potentially lethal attacks, Mobutu recognised that it would be in his best interests to negotiate a long-term peace with Angola. Congo agreed to withdraw support for anti-government rebels associated with the FNLA which might threaten the stability of the Luanda government. Mobutu thereby gave up, for the time being, any hope either of capturing the Cabinda oil wells or of helping to install in Luanda a government which would be friendly to his own brand of rampant capitalism, a capitalism in which private participation in business and industry by politicians was strongly favoured. Congo also hoped that peace with Angola might enable it to reopen the direct railway line from the Congo copper and cobalt mines to the Atlantic harbour at Lobito, thus greatly facilitating the traditional export of heavy minerals. Mobutu's peace proposals were accepted by the now ailing Agostinho Neto and Angola moved the Katanga *gendarmerie* back from the frontier while keeping it on standby for any future operations that might serve the government's strategic needs. The peace of 1978 made it possible for tens of thousands of Angolans to leave their adopted homes in western Congo and return to their ancestral homes in northern Angola. Their defeated military and political leaders slipped into the shadows of an unpublicised exile from which they only emerged fourteen years later when, after the end of the Cold War, the United Nations was able to bring temporary stability to Angola and organise a multiparty election for which all the surviving old guard politicians came home. Long before that, however, the 'old man' of Angolan politics, Agostinho Neto, was struck down with cancer. In 1979 he died in a Moscow hospital.

8

SURVIVAL IN THE EIGHTIES

The Angolan wars of liberation ended with the death of Agostinho Neto. Already, however, a new conflict was brewing which was once again both a civil and an international war. The key problem in understanding Angola's postcolonial history is that of why, after the protracted and blood-stained birth pangs of the liberation struggle, the country failed to settle down and tackle the conventional problems of economic and social development which were the normal legacy of colonialism. The causes of the new war of the 1980s were many. The role of the Soviet Union in Africa during its last ten years of existence is one factor and it may be significant that Angola's second president, José Eduardo dos Santos, was an engineer in the petroleum industry who had trained in Russia. Another long-distance factor that might be deemed important was the role of the United States which elected a president, Ronald Reagan, who adopted a virulently hawkish agenda during the Cold War confrontations of the decade. In the conflict between the United States and Russia one of the irritants was the political agenda of Cuba, which was anxious to build an international reputation of its own and, in the name of Third World freedom, provided extensive civilian and military support to the much-battered MPLA government of Angola. Over a fifteen-year period of rolling aid programmes, Cuba supplied Angola with cohorts eventually totalling 50,000 civilian teachers, doctors and bureaucrats as well as 200,000 military personnel.

At a more regional African level, the peace deal with Congo (temporarily known as Zaire) opened the way for the return to Angola of tens of thousands of old Kongo exiles. Making political and economic space for these returnees sometimes put strains on the fragile post-colonial government which was only slowly recovering from the virulent purges that had followed the attempted *coup d'état* of 1977. Meanwhile, on Angola's southern front, South Africa was still smarting from the humiliation of having been defeated in Angola in March 1976. Moreover South Africa was deeply threatened by political unrest within its own territory when, in June 1976, the students of Soweto rose up in rebellion, partly fired with enthusiasm by the liberation from white rule which Angolans had achieved. The same stirrings of revolution began to mobilise the liberation forces in Namibia, which launched an armed struggle against South Africa in order to win independence. They used Angola as a training ground for guerrillas and as a haven for asylum-seekers. The last unfinished agenda which brought pervasive grief to the peoples of Angola was the inability of the new government, led by dos Santos, to satisfy the legitimate aspirations of the southern élite of Angola's highland cities who had not been dealt an equitable hand in the settlements of the late 1970s. They remained isolated and aggrieved and therefore supported guerrillas on the remote south-eastern edge of the old Portuguese colonial world. The discontent of these southern peoples was probably the most important factor fuelling a war which lasted throughout the 1980s.

It was during the 1980s, beginning with the northern peace secured with Congo in 1978 and culminating in a southern peace agreed with South Africa in 1991, that Angola experimented with many political, diplomatic and economic survival strategies as the tide of war rose and fell in tandem with the politics of the Cold War—taking on a new intensity with the inauguration of Reagan as president of the United States in 1981 and diminishing with the gradual collapse of Gorbachev's Soviet Union after the breaching of the Berlin Wall in 1989. Angola's ruling élite earned money from the export of oil and, following international ideological shifts, moved from a Soviet style command-management in the early 1980s to an American style free-market in the late 1980s. All the while the South African ministry of defence perfected a policy of destabilisation directed against Angola. Cuba meanwhile persisted in raising the level of its military support for Angola, undeterred by Luanda's shift from socialism to capitalism. The great survivor of the political opposition was Jonas Savimbi who constantly trimmed his sails to the prevailing wind. He armed his guerrillas on the proceeds of diamonds dug from Angola's inland river beds.

The ending in 1978 of the old interventionist war between Angola and Congo brought about one of the most fundamental changes to postcolonial

Angola. This was the mass migration of exiles who returned from their havens in the formerly Belgian Congo to their ancestral homes in the formerly Portuguese sphere of influence in the old Kongo kingdom. The men and women who came back from Kinshasa, accompanied by a new generation of northern Angolans who had been born in exile in Congo, had to work hard to find new niches of opportunity. Some settled in the villages of the north and took up farming but life was hard, the plantation industry had collapsed, the white bush traders had gone, and a meagre level of subsistence could only occasionally be supplemented by smuggling consumer goods across the border from Congo in exchange for bags of wild coffee beans or bunches of cooking bananas. Such austerity had little appeal for returnees accustomed to a much higher standard of living. Thus it was that many returning exiles moved on to seek their fortunes in the yet unknown city of Luanda.

The transition from city life in Congo to the urban centre of Angola was equally fraught with difficulty. Power and status in Luanda depended on a firm grasp of the Portuguese language but the returning exiles from Kinshasa had been educated in French. They were treated as foreigners by the proud and clannish people of Luanda, just as they had formerly been treated as foreigners while living on the Belgian side of the border. While in Congo, immigrant and refugee 'strangers' from Angola had had no access to government employment but became expert at carving out economic space in the private sector. They acted as butchers' boys in the white-owned slaughter houses, became touts for taxi drivers, and sometimes even graduated to become drivers themselves. For some, petty trade was their mainstay, hawking shirts through the streets, minding barrows of produce from the countryside, staffing market stalls which sold everything from plastic sandals to kerosene-fuelled refrigerators. The Angolans who returned 'home' to Angola were not only the children of the northerners who had fled from the vigilante massacres of 1961 in the coffee groves. They were also the grandchildren of Angolans who had served the Belgians over three generations. They arrived in Angola with blue-collar skills which white-collar Creoles did not possess. They were seen, however, as 'strangers' without family networks to protect them and so they clung to each other, generating envy and suspicion among the native-born Luandans. The citizens of Luanda knew the workings of the public-sector employment which they inherited, but had no understanding of the commercial sector. Trade, even petty trade, had been in the hands of the departed Portuguese who had acted as cobblers and mechanics, hairdressers and barmaids, stall holders and bakers. The 'returnees' from Kinshasa identified opportunities which made them economically indispensable, though not popular, when they became the city's new trading community. The drive commonly possessed by migrants with no access to landed property, or salaried jobs, made entry into the risk-taking crafts and trades the only option. Officially the MPLA looked askance at the rapid rise of the private enterprises which the northerners established. In practice, however, welcoming the scarce skills in business offered by returnees was an important survival strategy for urban-dwellers, whose needs could not be satisfied by the poorly-supplied and inadequately-staffed official agencies. 'Parallel markets' run by 'Zairotas', as the Kinshasa returnees were scornfully dubbed, sprang up everywhere and soon even the most hard-line ideologues of the MPLA found they were compelled to join the ranks of free-market customers.

The wildly-uncontrolled market of postcolonial Angola had many interesting effects on survival strategies, including the relationship between the state sector, in the hands of the ruling party which operated a Soviet-style economy, and the private sector, managed by the northern returnees. State employees, Portuguese-speaking Angolans with government-sponsored jobs, received coupons which enabled them to buy a range of authorised goods, in state-owned supermarkets, at controlled prices. These government-issued rations, including good-quality imported whisky, could later be sold off at deregulated prices on the parallel market in exchange for all the goods which the planned economy could not supply—ranging from a fresh chicken to spare parts for a Mercedes. In the process of exchanging coupon goods for black-market goods, money virtually ceased to be recognised and barter became the recognised medium of exchange. The twenty-four-pack of lager beer in aluminium cans became the nominal, and often the physical, measure of exchange, serving as a bulky pseudo-currency. To buy an expensive item on the parallel market, one that cost more than a head-load of beer cans, it was necessary to rent a pickup truck to deliver the negotiated price in hard produce. For large payments, as in the buying and selling of urban real estate, the informal sector sometimes measured value in uncut diamonds, illicitly traded in match boxes. The free-market barter system in Angola was far from being whimsical since the pseudo-currency values were underpinned by the export price of oil. Prices on the black market shadowed the international price of oil accurately and speedily, like an economic barometer. The 'alternative' economy fuelled by Congo returnees who had abandoned the political agenda of the FNLA and had become the economic partners of civil and military MPLA personnel, may have been unorthodox but it was not unsubtle and its scale became gigantic in a city which had risen from half a million to several million inhabitants.

While returned exiles established a private commercial sector which enabled urban Angolans to live through the uncertainties of independence, in the countryside it was working women who bore the burden of the struggle for survival. Young men were constantly liable to be conscripted, or kidnapped, to serve in Angola's rival armies and it was therefore women, children and old men who were left to fend for themselves, inventing ever more imaginative economic strategies based on small-scale farming and petty barter. Survival in the villages of Angola was made enormously difficult by an almost continuous 'war of destabilisation' which gripped the country in the 1980s. Military planners in both UNITA and the MPLA were not averse to starving rural populations in order to drive them out of 'enemy' territory. Farm produce was a scarce strategic resource which could be used to sustain the opposing army. One cruel way of manipulating civilian populations was by laying minefields round farm-land and water sources. Women going out to their field, or children going down to the stream, were liable to have their legs blown off. The strategy maimed, rather than killed, many victims leaving the opposing society with the cost of feeding and caring for its crippled citizens.

Although counting unmapped minefields is difficult, it was roughly estimated that several million mines were laid in Angola to deny farmers access to land. Such a number made Angola's killing fields comparable to those of Cambodia. The plight of the largely female victims was publicised to the world by Princess Diana, to the dismay of a British government which had hitherto sold anti-civilian weapons of every variety almost indiscriminately, and highly profitably. The British princess visited the minefields, spoke to women in rehabilitation centres, and cuddled children fitted with wooden limbs. In the savagely brutalised central region of the Kwanza valley, MPLA home territory and a prime target for UNITA, women remained defiantly self-sufficient. When well-meaning aid-workers tried to establish marketing cooperatives, the women declined the proposal, saying that any formally-constituted organisation would fall prey to the politics of men. Men, it was widely believed, would consume the profits of any organised cooperative by converting the produce into alcohol and tobacco. Women alone could ensure that the fruits of farming reached the mouths of children.

Subsistence was the key to rural survival, but some market strategies were put in place on farms south of the Kwanza. An astute trader was able to take maize to market by adapting a child's scooter to carry a bag that was heavier than she could carry on her head. The wooden construction materials were entirely local and the frequently-needed repairs required no outside technology.

As on the push-bike trails of wartime Vietnam, peasants carried tons of farm produce over long distances to add some market opportunity to their survival strategies. When each spasm of the war subsided, male-owned trucks returned to rural districts to buy 'surplus' food in exchange for city goods for consumption or for barter. Some of the owner-drivers of bush lorries were erstwhile Portuguese settlers who returned to their former stamping grounds and to their traditional trading pursuits. Neither the self-help scooters, nor the old colonial lorries, were ever adequate, however, to feed the swelling towns or the huge encampments of displaced war victims. In some provincial towns a web of air bridges had to be built by philanthropic organisations which flew in food to prevent the rival armies from starving out their enemies. Down on the coast it was displaced women from the highland who showed the utmost ingenuity in creating market gardens in old white suburbs and in growing onions and cabbages in former colonial playgrounds. They also cultivated the central reservations of carriageways to plant maize and used water from standpipes in the shanties to irrigate tomatoes. Thus did Angolans eke out a precarious living during the endless rounds of war.

One of the economic enclaves in which women gained both wealth and prestige was Luanda fish-mongering. The fishing boats were traditionally owned by coastal men and crewed by workers from the highland, some of them Bailundu migrants. The selling of the fish had traditionally been the preserve of women, but in the late-colonial period white entrepreneurs had encroached on their domain and diverted the considerable wealth generated by the industry into the male sector of the economy. When whites fled from Angola at the prospect of a turbulent independence, black women recovered part of their niche in the fish market. They celebrated their wealth as queens of the Luanda carnival, the epitome of prestige among true city natives. Rich female fishmongers ostentatiously decked their granddaughters out in the finest costumes of the carnival dance brigades. Even in the years of the most acute wartime austerity women wholesalers were able, thanks to relatives serving as international seamen, to order textiles from Europe, America and Asia for the competitive carnival displays. So prestigious were the carnival queens that the suit-wearing men of the MPLA appropriated the festival for their own political purposes. Each year they used the carnival to celebrate the March anniversary of their victory over South Africa in 1976. Among the dance companies it was almost always one of the fishing guilds which won the supreme prize. Their defeated farming opponents were cast into a shadow of despair which they, and their menfolk, drowned in palm wine, cane brandy and alcoholic oblivion.

Under colonialism working-class women, white as well as black, had often been downtrodden. Middle-class colonial women, on the other hand, had gained social and economic freedoms in Angola which went far beyond those available in authoritarian Portugal. This tradition of emancipated opportunity carried through into the years of independence and some women sympathetic to the MPLA were offered such prestigious posts as university rector or national librarian. Even UNITA, the ultra-macho liberation movement, appointed a woman as one of its senior economic advisers. In government, some token women were appointed junior ministers, but none played a role in running the oil sector or managing the army. A party organisation for women appeared to put women on a pedestal while effectively removing them from real access to power. High-profile women were more likely to play a role in the dynastic politics of the Luanda families than in political power struggles. Women in authority were deemed an offence to male African pride, as the United Nations discovered when it appointed a very senior female peace broker to serve in Angola. Margaret Anstee, for all her astute diplomatic activity, found that her Nigerian military commander of the UN force was barely able to address a civil word to her, so offended had he been at the idea of serving a woman with real power. Jonas Savimbi was even more outraged, describing her in his wireless tirades as little better than a whore. President dos Santos, meanwhile, prided himself not only on having a former Russian wife, but also one who belonged to one of the great Creole dynasties.

Although women who farmed the land were the heroic survivors of the war in rural Angola, they were also some of the most abused victims of the male armies which endlessly trampled across the countryside throughout the 1980s. Attitudes to women, both in the MPLA war for liberation and in the UNITA war for destabilisation, are portrayed in two of Angola's prominent war novels, Pepetela's *Mayombe* and Sousa Jamba's *Patriotas*, in both of which frustrated conscripts fantasise about the supply of beautiful women whom their superior officers guarded for their own enjoyment. The colonial war of the 1960s had done nothing to protect Angolan women from predatory experiences and although the sexual activities which colonial conscripts indulged in were seen by some regime propagandists as evidence of racial toleration, they were actually the face of inhuman white arrogance. The long-term consequences were dire and the armies of the 1980s adopted the same predatory attitude to women as had the colonisers of the 1960s. One bombastic colonial officer had even proclaimed the hope that each white conscript would impregnate half a dozen African girls and so implant colonial culture in Angola by means of rape. The legacy brought intensified racial confrontation when some children of white fathers, whether legitimate or not, saw themselves as above other Angolans. In retaliation, true blackness was adopted by some politicians, including Savimbi, as a badge to proclaim superiority over the 'bastard' children of the Portuguese empire.

The well-being of the sophisticated élite which ruled Angola after the end of the liberation wars of the 1970s was enhanced throughout the 1980s by the growing supply of crude petroleum. The oil revenue cushioned Luanda from the austerity which the collapse of the colonial economy had inflicted on the countryside. It was also the economic fuel which made the war particularly ferocious. In Angola, as in Africa's other oil-producing nation, Nigeria, which had also been wracked by a postcolonial civil war, those who held the oil wells were unwilling to share their bounty with those who did not. The oil industry had begun to transform Angola in the last years of colonial rule, but after the fall of Portugal petroleum became the country's most important, indeed almost its only, source of export revenue. Unlike the formerly dominant agricultural economy, the oil industry was not an important source of employment generating salaried jobs or ancillary labouring work. Gulf Oil, renamed Chevron, serviced its Cabinda wells with American crews who came and went via French oil ports in Gabon, thus avoiding the effects of Angolan violence but leaving little positive mark on society other than the monthly payments to the government. These royalties grew during the 1980s as the great Atlantic oilfield spread south of the Congo River through the shallow waters of mainland Angola. When political conditions seemed right, new oil companies risked their venture capital in exploring blocks of concessions which stretched as far south as Luanda. Some companies even built on-shore facilities on the south bank of the Congo estuary, not far from the stone pillar erected in 1483 by an early explorer who wished to claim Angola for the Portuguese crown. It can be argued that it was oil which kept the several Angolan wars running for twenty-seven years. So long as the power-brokers of the city were unwilling to share the oil spoils, and recycle the national wealth in countrywide reconstruction, the politicians of south Angola refused to accept political or military defeat.

In Angola the centralisation of power was continually reinforced by oil revenue. Politicians who used oil royalties to pay for ever-more sophisticated weapons of war not only maintained their military advantage but also made substantial personal gains from bonuses and backhanders. City politicians creamed off the profits of oil and companies pumped the petroleum relatively unconcerned by the ebb and flow of traumatised war victims. The most corrupt of the politicians saw little advantage in ending the bloodshed, so long as they could close their hearts to the suffering in the provinces and rake in their personal bounty. The beneficiaries were kept on their toes by a constant game of musical chairs in which access to the benefits of office could be granted or withdrawn at a stroke of the presidential pen. The more tightly the owners of oil held on to their assets, the more open to Western corruption their political system became. This corruption was encouraged by every foreign interest, European as well as American. Expatriate businessmen and foreign politicians offered all conceivable types of illicit inducements in order to bypass any form of local consultation or any method of democratic accountability. Without any national auditing of oil revenue, the anger felt in the deprived provinces was all too understandable. Ironically it was foreign parties, some of whom were corrupting city politicians, who were also arming the rebellious provinces and stoking a war of destabilisation.

In 1985 there was a hiccup in the oil-fuelled war. This had less to do with the politics of Cold War interventionism and more with the need for the Angolan government to rethink its policies in the light of a drop in the international price of petroleum. Since 1979, when OPEC had negotiated a huge rise in the price of crude oil, Angola had been partially cushioned against any incompetence in its industrial planning system. The earnings from the colonial processing industries of the 1960s that had been nationalised, or confiscated, or simply abandoned, had been squandered in the first ten years of independence and manufacturing was down to little more than 30 per cent of former production levels. In 1980, an MPLA plenary congress had already recognised the problem but sought to put the blame for economic malfunction on individual speculation and administrative incompetence rather than on the theories adopted for the economic system. Until that time the government had more or less followed Soviet-style models of economic planning, though few if any of the leaders had much grasp of either the theory or the practice of Marxist-Leninism. Party members railed against embezzlement, illegal trading, inflation, unbridled corruption, unemployment, foreign debt, economic suffocation, poor education, and the failure of health services to fight both endemic and epidemic disease. They protested that the state had become parasitic. When the next party congress was called, in 1985, the crisis could no longer be blamed on individual failures. New ideological attitudes and administrative reforms were sought at a time of falling national income.

The crisis had bitten deep into the heart of Angola's central economic system and into the welfare of Luanda's peri-urban population which lived within sight of the affluent villas of the ruling élite. Economic decline was also leading to a serious brain drain. The departure of white technocrats and bureaucrats was followed by a crippling haemorrhage of black middle-class Angolans who left the country to seek job security and professional earnings abroad. Some went to more stable parts of the African continent but others went to Europe, including Portugal, and to North America. Trained and educated nationals who remained behind in Angola to work with the Cuban expatriates trying to keep industrial production and government services functioning, were constantly handicapped by shortages of imported raw materials, by an absence of spare parts for machines, and by frequent interruptions in the flow of water and electricity when storage dams and power stations were sabotaged by UNITA guerrillas.

The circular question of whether the war caused the economic decline or whether the economic decline was the cause of war could no longer be answered by blaming 'brigands', 'saboteurs' and 'opportunists' sponsored by Cold War protagonists. From 1985 a policy of 'economic purification' was therefore slowly embarked upon, leading to the introduction of at least some market principles and incentives. The mythical idea that Angola could plan for the development of heavy industry on a Stalinist model was dropped but any notion that light industry might be a viable form of economic diversification stumbled on the complete absence of a skilled workforce able to turn local raw material, even wood, into finished products. Equally difficult was the idea of reopening agriculture to the commercial sector. Civil servants and politicians had no concept of what risk-taking meant in the field of agrarian production and occasionally assumed, as had former planners in Eastern Europe, that workers could simply be directed into agriculture.

When reform of the economic production processes proved difficult, the government also embarked on a scheme for the purging of low and middle-level corruption. They were encouraged by Cuban advisers who had become sickened by the inefficiency that stymied all efforts to bring Angola out of its chaos. Gradually the beer-can system of barter was replaced by a twin currency with the local bank notes being used for soft-money transactions and American dollars employed for hard-currency purchases. Cracking down on the black market in uncut diamonds led to a degree of judicial ferocity in punishing those traffickers who were captured, but were unable to call on adequately powerful political friends to protect them. One senior Cuban commander without adequate political protection was taken home and shot for economic sabotage after allegedly being caught trading in diamonds, ivory, and ebony in exchange for hard currency and hard drugs. The adoption of market values, and of freely-traded currencies, may have facilitated the lives of those with access to valuable assets, but it put new pressures on the communities of displaced persons around the city. What is more, the economic reform programme did nothing to satisfy the aspirations of the southerners who continued to be excluded from new opportunities and so remained loyal to UNITA and to its leader.

Whether the war was largely fuelled by the frustrated ambitions of the UNITA leaders, or whether Jonas Savimbi was simply a puppet who opened Angola up as one of the convenient Asian, African and Latin American playgrounds on which the superpowers acted out their 'wars by proxy', is an intractable question. Without the Cold War, UNITA would probably not have survived, and southerners, like northerners, would have found a way to join the central bandwagon in the city. What made Angola different from Cold War confrontations in Nicaragua or Afghanistan was the presence on the southern border of the *apartheid* republic of South Africa, one of the most controversial pariah nations of the 1980s. The commitment of Angola, supported by Cuba, to freeing South Africa from the racial supremacy of its Afrikaans-speaking government, and the opposite commitment of South Africa to ridding Central Africa of a regime friendly to the 'evil empire' of the Soviet Union, gave the war of the 1980s an ideological edge. The war by proxy of the 1980s went beyond a domestic struggle for wealth and power, a struggle which was later revitalised during two civil wars in the 1990s. The key to Savimbi's survival from 1979, the year of the death of Agostinho Neto, to 1991, the year of the fall of the Soviet Union, was his alliance with the United States before, during, and after the Reagan presidency.

The US intervention in the Angolan wars of liberation had been largely ineffectual, and a subsequent reluctance to be publicly involved in foreign wars led the United States Congress, through the 1976 'Clark Amendment', to outlaw any sending of American weapons to the warring parties. Although the Carter administration, which took office in 1977, had a relatively liberal attitude in African affairs, and condemned South Africa for its repressive policies, it nevertheless remained a participant in the Cold War. Savimbi was discreetly permitted to visit Washington for talks with right-wing foreign policy experts such as Henry Kissinger. At the same time, corporate America remained keen to do business with the Angolan government, selling aircraft, electronic equipment, computers, and oil-drilling technology. When Reagan came to power in 1981 he was initially unable to persuade Congress to repeal the Clark Amendment, but he covertly fuelled the Angolan sector of the Cold War and vetoed attempts by the United Nations to restrain South Africa from ever-more frequent incursions into Angola. Although South Africa's attacks were nominally in pursuit of Namibian guerrillas fighting for the independence of their country, in practice many of the targets were Angolan army installations. Even more directly, and illegally, Reagan used third parties to arm Savimbi's southern guerrillas with weapons coming not directly from the US, but from Belgium, Switzerland, Israel and other American client states. The funding was channelled through Saudi Arabia and other Western trading partners. To facilitate the delivery of weapons to UNITA, a covertly managed Central Intelligence Agency charter firm won the air supply contract for Angola's official diamond mines. While legitimate supplies of mining equipment were thus carried, it was also possible to ferry illegitimate supplies to opposition units camped out beyond the diamond fields.

Although euphemistically described in the United States as a' low intensity' conflict, the pressure of war on Angola eventually became such that in February 1984 the Luanda government felt compelled to seek a truce with South Africa. Savimbi, however, wanted victory, not peace, and so immediately vitiated the South African deal and pounced on Luanda's largest hydroelectric plant with a terrorist attack. A few months later Reagan won his second term as president and rapidly stepped up his support for Savimbi's campaign to defeat the MPLA and win power for the southern coterie. Reagan used the slogan 'Africa has a right to be free' and got the Clark Amendment repealed thus enabling him to supply war materials to Angola in a legal, if unpublicised, manner. Savimbi was presented to the American public not as a 'freedom fighter' but as a champion of 'democracy' and in January 1986 he was invited to the White House. Thereafter UNITA fought its way out of the empty savanna plains of the southeast and back into the populated highland, where it could pressurise conscripts into joining its fighting force. Civilian deaths rose to hundreds of thousands as 'soft targets' were captured, defended and then recaptured by the opposing sides.

South Africa had borne the brunt of the effort to support Savimbi and topple dos Santos ever since its return to Angola in the years following its expulsion in 1976. The main public justification for returning was the forward defence of Namibia, the ex-German colony which South Africa had conquered in 1915 and still held in 1980 despite international resolutions which determined that the United Nations, and not South Africa, was the rightful custodian of Namibian sovereignty. South Africa feared that irregular companies of Namibian freedom fighters would attack its occupying army across the Cunene River. The guerrillas had set up camps in Angola when they failed to get Western opinion to condemn the illegitimate occupation by South Africa. Even Britain's Labour government was unwilling to jeopardise colonial stability in Namibia when oil prices rose and the industrial world became increasingly dependent on alternative nuclear energy for which Namibian uranium was one of the preferred fuels.

South Africa had an economic as well as a strategic agenda in Angola: it aspired to establish neo-colonial domination over a neighbour which, during the Portuguese colonial war, had been a valued ally. In order to restore 'harmonious' relations with Angola, South Africa had decided to 'destabilise' the government in the hope that when it fell it would be replaced by one that was more amenable to economic collaboration. One objective was the search for a supply of crude oil that would not be cut off by the economic sanctions imposed by suppliers hostile to *apartheid*. This search was made more urgent after 1979 when the pro-Western Shah of Iran, who had traditionally supplied South Africa's oil, was overthrown. Another South African ambition was to widen the market for South African exports, both agricultural food-stuffs and manufactured consumer goods, at a time when boycotts were threatening traditional markets. Existing markets in Congo and Zimbabwe were too small to compensate for the lack of purchasing power of domestic black consumers inside South Africa.

International relations were important to South Africa, which needed to maintain good relations with the United States. So long as there was a Soviet presence in Angola, South Africa could always claim that it was a bulwark against Soviet global expansionism and Russian neo-colonialism. While Angola hosted an expeditionary army from Cuba, South Africa could also continue to play effectively on American fears that Cuban ideas of 'freedom' were being exported beyond the shores of the beleaguered island which American governments had for so long, and so fiercely, demonised. By playing up the danger of Soviet influence in central Angola, and by allowing its army to hold down the Cuban force in southern Angola, South Africa safeguarded itself from American interference in its domestic political agenda of segregation and repression. Whenever a Washington lobby, whether white or black, demanded sanctions against South Africa, in order to hasten the advent of democracy, Pretoria only had to point to the Russian 'menace' for the appeal to be brushed aside and the alliance between the United States and South Africa to be reaffirmed.

The changes which came to Angola in the late 1980s were brought about by a series of mutations in geopolitical relations. At the economic level, a fall in the price of world energy meant that uranium was no longer such a precious asset and the western members of the United Nations no longer felt the need to protect South Africa's occupation of Namibia and thereby risk incurring the ire of liberal or black members of their electorates. At a strategic level, South Africa found that it no longer had the military capacity to carry on the war. The war had escalated from savannah skirmishes into a battle over a hard target, the former Portuguese military base of Cuito Cuanavale, held by the MPLA and the Cubans. The battle lasted for months and the cost in both men and materials escalated. The Cuban contingents in Angola reached 50,000 men and the MPLA war debt in Moscow reached a billion dollars. It was South Africa, however, which was forced to call a halt to the hostilities after the loss of irreplaceable French Mirage jets. South Africa also realised that the death of white conscripts could no longer be hidden by press censorship from the voting public.

The battle of Cuito Cuanavale, coming as it did at the end of the Cold War, had repercussions both for defeated South Africa and for victorious Angola. Namibia won its independence and so the issue of guerrilla camps on Angolan territory ceased to be relevant. The South African army lost its prestige at home and its key supporter, President Botha, fell from office, opening the way to a new era of reform and eventually to democracy. The Cuban army agreed to withdraw from Angola and could do so with its head held high after its success against a previously invincible South African army. In the United States, the hard-line regime of Ronald Reagan gave way to the slightly less doctrinaire one of George Bush senior, the old spymaster who back in 1976 had once withdrawn the CIA from Angola. The Soviet Union disbanded its empire in Europe and surrendered most of its interests in Africa.

The plethora of changes that affected Africa at the end of the 1980s brought real hope that without foreign interventions peace might at last be possible in Angola. The end of the Reagan era, the winding down of the Soviet Union, and the implementation of a peace treaty between South Africa and Cuba, did not, however, bring lasting peace. Despite all efforts, the domestic causes of the Angolan conflict were to resurface after the Cold War had ended. In June 1989 President Mobutu of Zaire, anxious to win favour with Washington, tried to broker an Angolan peace by inviting dos Santos and Savimbi to his great palace at Gbadolite, where the war leader from the highland and the war leader from the city were tricked into meeting for the first time and frigidly shook hands. Seven days later Savimbi's commandoes destroyed the Luanda electricity supply. In retaliation dos Santos's army launched an attack on Mavinga, the gateway to the rutted bush trails which led to Savimbi's remote south-eastern encampment at Jamba. The United States felt temporarily compelled to re-enter the war with an airlift of weapons to save Savimbi from being ejected by Soviet-equipped forces. In March 1990, however, representatives of the United States and Russia met face to face at the Namibia independence ceremony in Windhoek. They negotiated their own terms for ending the Cold War in the Angolan theatre. A year later, in May 1991, the Angolans themselves reluctantly signed a ceasefire at Bicesse in Portugal after losing their Cold War patrons. This peace was to be monitored by the United Nations, which sent Margaret Anstee, a former deputy to the secretary-general, to supervise Angola's first ever democratic election. Down in the Luanda slums the 1991 accord was gratefully known as 'Margaret's peace'.

9

CIVIL WAR AND THE COLONIAL AFTERMATH

When Angola came out of the Cold War in 1991 it was a different country from the one that had emerged from the colonial war. In 1974, a major export had been coffee, efficiently carried by lorry on asphalted highways built for strategic military purposes. In 1991 one of the exports which exceeded coffee was scrap metal, quarried from the half-a-million tonnes of non-ferrous junk attached to the thousands of military and civilian vehicles which had been blown up along Angola's ruined roads during the years of bitter conflict. The graveyard of military vehicles was matched by the graveyard of human victims. Those who had died of hunger, wounds, disease or gunshots were buried and uncounted, but those who survived—maimed, crippled, displaced and unemployed—were all too visible to the agencies which supplied them with basic meals and artificial limbs.

When the burdens of war were temporarily lifted, the eighteen months from May 1991 to September 1992 were the most spectacular period of optimism and freedom that Angola had ever witnessed. Savimbi and his entourage of generals moved up from their remote fastness at Jamba to establish opulent residential quarters in the Miramar district of Luanda, overlooking the palm-fringed bay. Thousands of highland refugees, camped in the coastal cities, loaded their meagre possessions on to their heads and set off for the interior to rediscover their villages and seek out surviving relatives. International observers poured into the country to marvel at the peace process, at the new economic opportunities, and at the adoption in Africa of a democratic procedure to settle differences. The political parties hired public relations firms to run sophisticated election campaigns on television, and the political leaders drew large crowds of cheering supporters to their rallies in town squares across the country. The UN representative, Margaret Anstee, flew everywhere in decrepit aircraft, parsimoniously funded by the United States and courageously piloted by intrepid Russians. She endeavoured to harmonise the two partisan armies that were to be partly demobilised and partly integrated into a single national force. The euphoria of peace, however, made supervised demobilisation virtually impossible. The government conscripts vanished into civilian society while the opposition ones were sometimes hidden away in provincial redoubts in case the 'leader' should require their services later. The most obsolete of UNITA weapons were handed over to teams of international inspectors but sophisticated military equipment was apparently cached in arms dumps strategically chosen around the provinces by Savimbi himself. On the government side a new security force, dressed in a sinister black costume, was armed and trained for action against civilians, should circumstances lead to urban warfare after the election. While people danced in the streets and vowed that war should never return, the pragmatic power-brokers on both sides made contingency plans.

After a year of blissful peace, Angola finally went to the polls to elect a parliament and a new president. In the election voters were broadly divided cleanly between those in the towns and those in the countryside. Several towns had more or less survived the war of destabilisation with imported food bought with oil revenue. The countryside had done much less well. The Soviet-style economy had failed to create a rural network that could purchase produce from farmers or distribute essential commodities such as soap, salt and cooking oil. The difference was striking when, on 12 September 1992, the countryside voted for the opposition, for Savimbi and for change, while the towns voted for the government, for subsidised food, and for protection against hungry raiders from the rural areas. UNITA leaders were dismayed to find that many urban Ovimbundu, both in highland towns and in coastal cities, had failed to support them but had adopted the urban strategy of voting for the MPLA. Equally dismaying to Savimbi was the betrayal by the United States, which had allegedly promised him that if he were to stop the war, and go to the polls, he would win the election. When Savimbi failed to prevail, by a clear margin of two to one in the parliamentary election and by a decisive, though not absolute, majority vote for the presidency, he prepared to return to war. Western-style democracy had no consolation prize for coming second in first-past-the-post, winner-takes-all, voting. Savimbi refused to contemplate a compromise solution, recognising that the presidential system, so attractive to him when he thought he would win, gave all power to the president rather than to a prime minister, or a cabinet, or an elected parliament. He calculated that his only hope of gaining the power which he had craved pathologically since his student days in Switzerland, was to seize it through the barrel of a gun.

Civil war broke out in Angola on 1 November 1992 and was different from the colonial war of 1961, from the interventionist war of 1975, and from the destabilisation war of the 1980s. All three of the earlier conflicts had been fought primarily in the countryside and had only indirectly affected towns. The war of 1992 concerned whole cities. The defeated opposition could do its electoral sums as effectively as any United Nations observer and recognised that it was in the urban heartland that it had lost its bid for power. UNITA therefore set out to destroy disloyal cities. It also set out to destroy, if possible, a government that had proved itself unwilling to make any concessions to its opponents or even offer significant post-war redistribution of the national wealth. The civil war of 1992 broke out initially in Luanda itself, triggered by UNITA's intransigent rejection of the election result, but launched with vigour by the government. Within days the city was violently cleansed of politicians unwilling to abandon Savimbi's cause. Worse still urban militias were given licence to settle old scores and attack townspeople who might have been less than loyal to the government.

The conflict of 1992–94 brought heavier weapons to Angola than the ones used in previous wars. Big towns of the interior such as Huambo and Malange were shelled as the population starved. Savimbi no longer received weapons from South Africa but had access to relatively cheap second-hand equipment bought, ironically, from the former Soviet empire. The huge republic of Ukraine, with 50 million people struggling to make a living, sold him redundant military hardware and its air fleet flew weapons, ammunition and fuel-oil to makeshift airstrips hidden in the orchard savannah of eastern Angola. Payment for the new UNITA arsenal was made by digging diamonds from the rivers of the interior and flying them, via cloak-and-dagger channels, to Antwerp, the capital of the diamond world, or to new diamond-cutting centres in Tel Aviv and Mumbai. In the expensive business of modern warfare, fought with technologically sophisticated weapons requiring imported ammunition, UNITA came to recognise that its diamond wealth was small compared to the oil wealth of the government. In 1993 it therefore attacked an on-shore oil installation at the mouth of the Congo River, either to deprive the MPLA of revenue or to capture an oil supply of its own. The oil port of Soyo temporarily fell into opposition hands but ruptured storage tanks only caused massive pollution while the oil platforms on the ocean horizon were never at risk. Savimbi was forced to recognise that early military successes had exhausted his resources and could bring no immediate political victory. For survival he needed to seek a truce.

Ending the civil war proved a particularly intractable diplomatic challenge. Margaret Anstee, having orchestrated the election with aplomb, negotiated valiantly to win the peace. It was not until late in 1994, however, that a new United Nations peacemaker, Alioune Beye, eventually secured an agreement in Lusaka. The accord generated none of the euphoria that had accompanied the peace signed in 1991. Savimbi showed his contempt for the unpalatable necessity of suspending hostilities by staying away from the signing ceremony. He had no desire to come face-to-face with dos Santos, who had now outwitted him both in an election, which had been patently free and fair, and in siege warfare, which had given the government control of the highland cities that Savimbi deemed to be his birth-right. Savimbi retired to the small highland town of Bailundu to plot future political and military developments. Dos Santos set about consolidating his personal power by both political and financial means. Savimbi evaded all forms of United Nations peace monitoring under the terms of the Lusaka Protocol while dos Santos basked in almost unlimited Western support. War remained on the horizon, however, and each side tried to provoke the other into being the first to break the ceasefire and so incur international opprobrium. The cold hostility, neither war nor peace, lasted for four years.

One way in which the president sought to defuse the anger of the opposition, and minimise the danger of a return to war, was by creating a 'government of national unity'. A number of posts were offered to members of the southern élite who were willing to leave the highland and join the ruling circle in Luanda. Some seventy UNITA members who had been elected to parliament in September 1992 moved to the comforts of the city and took their seats in the legislative chamber. Seven of their leaders became ministers and vice-ministers in a cabinet whose padded payroll included sixty MPLA members. Some highland generals were apparently offered inducements of 3 million US dollars each to change sides. The relatively low-key concession to power-sharing was silently undermined, however, by the continuing rise of presidential authority.

The failure of the 1992 election, and the catastrophic war which followed, convinced President dos Santos that he must concentrate more power in his own hands. From being a single-party state with a disaffected opposition thinly scattered in the provinces, Angola became a presidential state in which power emanated from the palace. Dos Santos, like Louis XIV, built his palace on the outskirts of the restless city, safely removed from the fickle mob, and it was there that political decisions began to bypass ministries, party cells, and bureaucracies. Angola was no longer a 'people's republic' and the president's huge, well-fortified, residential complex, known as the Futungo, resembled the ostentatious luxury displayed by Mobutu in Zaire in contrast to the austere highland hideouts in which Savimbi dodged from night to night to avoid assassination by his many personal and political foes. For all the gilding on his cage, dos Santos was almost as much a prisoner as Savimbi since he was reluctant to travel through the country, even accompanied by his heavily-armed guard. The caged president orchestrated a personality cult with adulation for the man of peace, a shining contrast with Savimbi, the warmonger. The presidential court even suggested that dos Santos, who had been at war with his own people for twenty years, be nominated for the Nobel Peace Prize!

In 1998 the presidential personality cult reached a climax during a week-long birthday party for dos Santos. He ceremonially visited the restoration work on the seventeenth-century chapel of Our Lady of Muxima, launched a regatta and a parachuting competition, awarded new costumes to paramount chiefs, and unveiled a commemorative postage stamp. He also opened an exhibition on 'protecting the sea and its riches' to show his concern for the environment though many of his human subjects went on starving. The medical plight to which the country had been reduced gave the president an opportunity to visit favoured hospitals bearing gifts, to call on a leper colony, and on a camp for displaced children. He expressed solidarity with those who campaigned against polio or sustained the victims of AIDS. An American-style fundraising dinner was devoted to the rehabilitation of the victims of landmines which his government had done as much as Savimbi's opposition to scatter over the country. The week-long festivities ended with gymnastics, sporting competitions, the cutting of a birthday cake and the award of a Brazilian honorary degree. Bread-and-circuses were an attempt to overcome popular disaffection and increasing fear of police surveillance. As the president became all-powerful even the elders of the MPLA felt marginalised, as when a prime minister from the prestigious van Dunem Creole family was humiliatingly made to carry the blame for government unpopularity. While people on the street saw the junketing and partying as an extravagant display of scandal and corruption, members of the establishment saw hero-worship as the necessary gateway to power and status. Money poured into the presidency and the politics of clientelism became ever more pronounced.

To sweeten those on whom the regime depended the presidential office increased the range of organisations which became dependent on its bounty and were therefore trapped into silent complicity. Benefactions were used both to minimise grass-root protest from the hungry slums and to manipulate the factionalism which kept the traditional cadres of the MPLA in disarray. One institutionalised step on the road to totalitarian presidentialism was the creation, in 1996, of the Eduardo dos Santos Foundation. This foundation was designed to implement a widespread policy of privatising the assets of the state so that they could be used to consolidate the power of the president rather than meet any of the more objectively assessed political needs of the nation. The ideology was far from new to Africa but in Angola the process was masked by opaque layers of secrecy and cloaked in dubious forms of legality. The patrimonial foundation refined the politics of patronage and derived its wealth from a presidential 'tax' which mirrored state taxes levied on international trading firms, petroleum prospectors, construction companies, and banking corporations as well as on the smaller domestic businesses. Having creamed off a top slice of the nation's assets, the foundation began to provide services that had ceased to be available through state channels but which now became privately accessible to the president's clients. A well-funded presidential university was set up to compete with the national university which had been named after Agostinho Neto. The foundation also gained public credit by giving a small subsidy to a home for abandoned children, though the core funding was siphoned out of the city council budget. Some of the largesse reached the provinces but presidential bounty was predominantly spent in the capital, the political base with a capacity to make or unmake presidents.

Manipulating power by wielding carrots and sticks for the élite was rather easier than winning support among the urban masses for whom poverty was a perceived consequence of widespread corruption. It became necessary to generate 'spontaneous' outbursts of popular enthusiasm for the president. The sans-culottes of Sambizanga, the black quarter in which dos Santos had been born but in which Nito Alves had mounted his 1977 challenge to the government of Agostinho Neto, were persuaded to come down into the asphalt town and demonstrate their loyalty to the president. The 'spontaneity' had been so well prepared that the chanting crowds wore specially prepared T-shirts bearing pictures of 'their' president. The mobilisation of the dispossessed rapidly grew bitter, however, when the crowds were permitted to search out approved public enemies against whom to vent their rage over their shabby poverty. The first permitted target was an ethnic one and the demonstrators chanted anti-Ovimbundu slogans as they intimidated anyone who had come down from the highland. In order to separate the faithful from the faithless it was suggested in parliament that identity cards should be issued naming the 'tribe' of each bearer, but this calamitous recipe for urban warfare was not followed up. By 1996 the orchestrated politics of violence were extended to include xenophobia and crowds were permitted to attack anyone who might be branded as 'foreign'. A government campaign against aliens was given the chilling code-name 'Cancer One' and the search for enemies was directed not only at Africans, particularly 'Zaireans' from Congo, but also at communities such as the Lebanese whom the population saw as exploiting shopkeepers.

While politicians were manipulating power down in the city, the highland was getting ready for war. By the end of 1996 it was estimated that Savimbi's war chest had grown to $2 billion and that he had recently been able to buy another 45 tonnes of weapons flown in from Bulgaria to the mile-long airstrip which UNITA conscripts had built near Bailundu. At this time no fewer than 20,000 of Angola's government troops were being tied down in Cabinda where armed secessionist movements were threatening the security of the oil wells. Each movement in the enclave had the potential to secure active support from Angola's northern neighbours, Congo-Brazzaville and Congo-Kinshasa, either of which would gladly have conquered Cabinda. On 17 May 1997 foreign relations suddenly changed, however, when Mobutu's dictatorship collapsed. A new military dictator, Laurent Kabila with a shadowy past in the Lumumba era, took control of Kinshasa and formed an alliance with the dos Santos government in Luanda. As a result of the change some 10,000 of Savimbi's troops, who had been sheltered by Mobutu, were temporarily stranded and had to seek refuge across the river in Congo-Brazzaville.

Within weeks of the Kinshasa revolution a similar revolution broke out in Brazzaville. To ensure an outcome that did not threaten Angola, dos Santos, with the tacit connivance of France and the United States, sent troops from Cabinda to support a former Brazzaville president, Sassou-Nguesso. In Brazzaville the regional logistics of civil war took on new dimensions with Croatian mercenaries on one side and weapons from Uzbekistan on the other. This turbulence disrupted UNITA's war preparation, but during 1998 Savimbi retrieved his scattered units, recruited some members of Mobutu's former presidential guard, and mobilised a force of 15,000 combat-ready men backed up by 10,000 auxiliary conscripts, a few genocidal Rwanda militants, the orphaned units which had lost power in Brazzaville, and a few Serbian mercenaries. Morocco had meanwhile trained a new officer corps to replace the UNITA generals who had been seduced into moving to Luanda.

Dos Santos also prepared for war after the accidental death on 18 June 1998 of the United Nations peacekeeper, Alioune Beye. Thirty battalions were deployed around the country and an air force equipped with Brazilian jet fighters was put on standby near Benguela. Spanish counter-insurgency specialists were brought in to train 25,000 police commandos who might be needed to repress civilian unrest once the war was launched. Luanda politicians hoped quickly to drive the UNITA forces out of the country and across the border into Zambia. City generals also aspired to capture the Kwango valley where UNITA's most plentiful alluvial diamonds had been found. By the last weeks of 1998 dos Santos was persuaded that further delay in attacking UNITA would be strategically foolish, but it was already too late to strike the winning blow and government forces, some inappropriately armed and others inadequately trained, were fiercely repulsed when they tried to take the highland. During the first half of 1999 UNITA held the military advantage and even its reluctant recruits, kidnapped from nominally 'friendly' Ovimbundu territory, fought for their lives, terrified by threats that if they lost the war the *mestizos* of the city would pack them off as despised farm labour to the greatly feared, snake-infested, forests of the northern lowland. The civil war of 1998 was the most cruel yet and humanitarian food supplies could not be flown to starving cities under siege.

The depraved conflict between a corrupt government mesmerised by wealth, and an inhuman opposition obsessed by power, carried on throughout 1999 and into 2000. In some engagements UNITA captured government weapons, but a shortage of fuel caused it serious logistical difficulties. One solution was to buy diesel covertly from the enemy. Personal relations across the divide between the two warring élites were closer than ethnic or ideological enmity might suggest. Successive peace negotiations had accustomed rival delegations to making deals with each other while drinking together in expensive foreign night clubs. But to buy fuel on a black market run by enemy officers required a supply of fresh diamonds. In the late 1990s it was estimated that as many as 100,000 men and women were being forced to dig the alluvial mud of the Kwango River for meagre returns of ever-smaller gems. Angola's diamonds earned barely one-tenth of the $7 billion a year now derived from oil, but they nevertheless enabled UNITA to continue operations after Cold War funding had been cut off. The leaders used diamond money to win support from France's client regimes in Burkina Faso, Togo and Côte d'Ivoire, all of which provided travel documents and forged sales papers. While the United Nations attempted, unsuccessfully, to impose penalties on nations which engaged in the diamonds-for-weapons trade, mercenary planes continued to fly diamond-funded guns into highland Angola. The weapons arrived under cover of darkness, relayed at unsupervised airstrips in countries which were rewarded for closing their eyes. When oil prices were low the government, like its opponents, struggled to fund the costs of warfare although it had managed to write off 4 billion of its old 11-billion-dollar war-debt. When oil prices recovered, however, the military tide turned and Savimbi lost his highland headquarters in Bailundu. Thereafter fighting concentrated on the dry, empty, plains on the eastern border through which the leader drove his mobile command caravan, visiting his shifting guerrilla camps.

With increasing oil prices an international scramble to obtain a stake in the Angolan petroleum industry reached gold-rush proportions. The exploration companies, those of Britain and France to the fore, calculated that the North Sea and Alaskan fields would run out of accessible reserves in the new century and that the best future prospects might lie in the ultra-deep concessions off Angola's Atlantic coast. Although the technology had not yet been perfected to drill oil from a seabed 2 miles deep—with underwater stations serviced by automated submarines and with flexible extraction pipes attached to surface platforms—the companies were nonetheless willing to make down-payments of $300 million for the right even to explore, let alone exploit, each block in Angola's deep waters. In the early months of the new millennium Luanda's 'jungle capitalism' was once more awash with money. The benefits of wealth did not, however, trickle down to the people. School teachers continued to be outnumbered by soldiers in a ratio of two-and-a-half to one. One-fifth of the national education budget was appropriated to educate élite children abroad. Voices of complaint, including those of independent Luanda newspapers, were silenced by government as brutally as the opposition had previously silenced Huambo journalists. In the countryside 'totalitarian savagery' continued unabated with the kidnapping of all available children for military duty. While slaughter ravaged the highland, members of Savimbi's family were sheltered in a West African haven controversially afforded them by the president of Togo.

By the year 2000 Angola had come full circle in the thirty years since the death of Salazar. The civil wars of the 1990s, like the colonial wars of the 1960s, had reached a stalemate. The lives of many people were disrupted but no solution to the military confrontation between the central government and the guerrillas seemed in sight. The economy had changed from a dependence on the unpredictable price of coffee to a dependence on the equally-fluctuating price of petroleum. In neither case was the industrial sector of production able to cushion the country against the uncertainties of world markets. Politics in 2000 was as unresponsive to public opinion as it had been in 1970, though the dictator who balanced the powers of the several factions of the property-owning class was now a member of Luanda's home-grown élite rather than of Portugal's imperially-oriented *haute bourgeoisie*. Now, as then, the army kept an eye on political decision-making and had a finger in the economic pie. Senior officers in the colonial army of the 1960s used their black market wealth to invest in real estate in Lisbon. The officers of the national army of the 1990s invested their newly-acquired riches in the Luanda housing market. Wealth was as sharply polarised as it had been in late-colonial times but the city slums had grown far beyond half a million with the arrival of 2 million displaced transients camped on the Luanda coastal plain. The colonial class of 200,000 privileged and semi-privileged expatriates had been replaced by a similar number of black Portuguese-speaking Angolans who retained many of the old colonial attitudes of social superiority and who worshipped in the same Catholic churches that had sustained Salazar's brand of authoritarianism. Dos Santos even invited the pope to visit Luanda and had one of his sons baptised a Catholic. On the streets the Angolan press of the 1990s was almost as circumscribed in its news and opinions as the censored press of the 1960s had been and Angolan citizens who held political views were as wary of the political police as colonial subjects had been when trying to evade Salazar's secret agents. Freedom of opinion and of opportunity, which had been stifled in the days of empire, appeared almost incapable of resuscitation in the era of liberation, though a few courageous voices such as that of journalist and human rights activist Rafael Marques could occasionally be heard. Some change was, however, afoot.

On 22 February 2002 Jonas Savimbi, the life-long commander of UNITA, was cornered, killed and secretly buried near the eastern town of Luena. The way was thereby opened for another attempt to find a peaceful future for Angola. Previous peace settlements drawn up at Bicesse in 1991, and Lusaka in 1994, had been orchestrated by foreigners and had failed. A new solution to the twenty-seven years of civil war, which had followed the thirteen years of colonial war, was drafted by Angolans themselves. Representatives of both liberation movements agreed on a peace formula so that the challenge of reconstruction could be faced. The parties were not, however, presented with a clean slate and the colonial legacy which they inherited was a deeply scarred one.

The complex reality of post-war Angola can only be understood by referring to its past. Well-meaning visitors, in the dawn years of the twenty-first century, rushed in talking about a 'return to normality', but this represented a failure to grasp history. Three-quarters of Angola's population had never known peace, last seen forty years before. The 'normality' of peace-time was entirely novel not only for young Angolans but also for most adults. As for democracy—that 'normality' embedded in the minds of Europeans—Angola had never enjoyed democracy. Indeed the one attempt to hold a one-person-one-vote election in Angola, the election of 1992, had resulted in one of the most destructive of all the wars that had torn the country apart. Angolans who had never known peace or democracy had never known the rule of law either. The institutions of political decision-making, and the administrative practices of the 2002 'government of reconciliation', were the unhappy linear descendants of a colonial police-state founded 100 years earlier by soldiers such as Paiva Couceiro and Norton de Matos and then ruled for forty years by Salazar. 'Administration by consent', or 'trial by jury', or 'participatory local government', were norms of an open society which the colonial powers had conspicuously failed to introduce into Africa. The long era of endemic warfare made a change of political style even more difficult to achieve in Angola than in former British or French colonies.

One pervasive war-time legacy was the widespread survival of anti-personnel land-mines strewn, unmapped, across Angola's farm lands. Clearing the mines was a highly skilled and very expensive operation, helped by such organisations as the Mines Advisory Group and the Halo Trust. One of Angola's own sophisticated de-mining experts had been trained in Cambodia where, as in Angola, millions of mines had been planted to starve peasants and to deprive towns of food. The clearing of the mines, however, did not necessarily benefit returning peasants who found that traditional titles to land-use were being challenged by entrepreneurs coming out from the city. The farms of the Amboim plateau, a mere hundred miles south of Luanda, were a particular target for demobilised generals who wanted to dust off colonial projects and re-establish plantations worked by cheap migrant labour. Absentee city millionaires also cast covetous eyes on the highland around Huambo. Land with good fertility, and in some cases with colonial irrigation and drainage, did not always return to Ovimbundu peasants with ancient oral rights. It was seized, instead, by carpet-baggers waving paper titles obtained from a corrupt and cash-starved bureaucracy.

The crisis over post-colonial land tenure was equally severe in Luanda. The old colonial suburbs of the city, the workers' town known as the *Bairo Operário*, had been built of brick to house those serving the public institutions. When the war ended, oil wealth enabled new city magnates to demolish even the best of the old boroughs to build high-rise apartment blocks. Housing was both for the victors of the civil wars and for the now increasing expatriate population. American oil companies, Brazilian engineering firms, Portuguese bankers, and great cohorts of foreign diplomats paid handsomely to live on the land being seized from its historic owners. The swathes of destruction by bulldozer were fiercely but unavailingly opposed. Dispossessed citizens were unable to wade through the jumbled piles of municipal archives to retrieve the title deeds to the houses and lands which they had lost. In the twenty-first century, outer suburbs were also being built by a neo-imperial generation of Chinese entrepreneurs. Public services, however, did not match urban growth. In the slums the *musseque* dwellers lacked water and sanitation and suffered health risks of plague proportions, but even middle-class Luandans regularly lacked piped water, reliable electricity, or collective transport. The city became so choked by private traffic that the president, with his cavalcade of out-riders, found the suburban bottle-necks so frustrating that he moved his office out of the suburbs and back to the city on high ground next to the cathedral.

One of the multi-facetted legacies of colonialism in Angola was Christianity. In the western regions the old Protestant traditions, Presbyterian, Methodist and Baptist, survived. In the east the Plymouth Brothers maintained a presence among war-time refugees. Foreign religious organisations brought health facilities to the most neglected of the provinces in an attempt to reduce infant and maternal mortality. Some Catholic voices had been brave enough to speak out against the brutality of civil war and one bishop was even awarded an international prize for defending civil rights. After the end of the war, Radio Ecclesia, a Catholic broadcasting station, became the most courageous voice of the independent media in Angola. A nervous government, however, insisted on curbing outspoken debate and closed the relay broadcasting stations which Britain had gifted to the provincial capitals in an effort to stimulate grass-roots democracy. The regime still saw rural rebellion as a possible threat to peace. Although fearful of the radical voice of Catholicism, the postwar government liked the power of an episcopal hierarchy and organised a pilgrimage to the old shrine of Muxima on the Kwanza River. 70,000 pilgrims travelled there by bus while some members of the élite chartered helicopters.

An equally dramatic religious development was an explosion of new churches in the Pentecostal tradition. After the war the Pentecostals bought up empty shops, hotels and warehouses and turned them into churches and chapels at the rate of one new congregation each week. Great preachers gave comfort to the masses and one prayer meeting filled a football stadium to its 80,000 capacity. The Pentecostals, with financial help from Brazil, were even able to build a cathedral-like church in Luanda. Alongside the growth of new Pentecostalism and of old Catholicism, Luanda city also preserved its Methodist core. The great Methodist church was regularly thronged under the auspices of an elderly black bishop who had survived all the phases of the wars. Some refugees returning from exile in Congo switched their allegiance from the Baptist Church to Methodism and sang the great Wesleyan hymns in Kikongo rather than in Kimbundu.

One of the controversial legacies of colonialism remained the off-shore oil economy which generated billions of dollars of revenue. In the tiny oil-producing enclave of Cabinda separatist political movements continued to wage war long after the rest of the country had secured peace. In 2010 their guerrillas even targeted a bus-load of footballers from Togo, captained by a Tottenham Hotspur star, as the team prepared to play in an Africa Cup match. The big question which the government of post-war Angola faced was whether the long-lauded presence of oil was really a blessing or actually a curse. As production rose from one million to two million barrels a day, first-world donor countries, such as Britain, deemed Angola rich enough to finance its own development priorities. The expected 'peace dividend', derived from the drop in military expenditure, now needed to be matched by a 'transparency dividend' which traced the flow of petroleum income. A bare 8 per cent of the government's oil revenue went into the key sectors of health and education. A similar proportion, perhaps as much as a billion dollars a year, allegedly escaped the purview of auditors and was apparently embezzled by top politicians who invested their winnings in Brazil, or stored them in Swiss banks. The task of auditing oil revenue was made particularly difficult when the drilling companies furtively failed to reveal how much oil they were extracting while the presidency stubbornly refused to reveal how much it was secretly charging each company for a drilling licence. Strict transparency would have been required to obtain development loans from the International Monetary Fund. Instead the president turned to more expensive credit from China, a country which studiously avoided political interference in the affairs of partner states and attached no moral strings to its investments. Angola, tragically, joined the oil-rich dictatorships of Uzbekistan and Equatorial Guinea as one of the most corrupt countries in the world. The problem of oil dependency grew more acute when in 2015 oil prices dropped. The government adopted harsher attitudes to its critics, notably the human rights lawyer and journalist Raphael Marques.

One obvious colonial legacy was the continued use of the colonial language. Indeed, an attempt to bridge ethnic boundaries after the war ended, and to create a distinctive cultural unity for the nation, was undertaken when the president declared that Portuguese would be the 'national'—not merely the 'official'—language of all Angolans. As one of the 'Lusophone' nations, Angola could be proudly contrasted with Francophone Congo and Anglophone South Africa. The continued use of the imperial language also facilitated a new relationship between the old colony and its former imperial master, a legacy which might not have been anticipated. A new form of 'neo-colonialism' enabled rich Angolans to buy up utility companies, telecommunications, and banks in the former mother country. As a result of such investments one of the president's daughters became the first female billionaire in Africa. Another feature of the association was the ability of Angolan businessmen to hire *Gastarbeiter* from Portugal who came to Angola with skills which were not available locally. This unexpected and reverse dependency on investment, and on migration, may have been hurtful to Portuguese pride, but it did help Portugal survive the 2008 economic crisis in the Eurozone. In Angola, meanwhile, after two centuries of colonial exploitation, people were at last in a position to visualise a stable and prosperous future and even benefit from their long relationship with Portugal.

In the early years of the twenty-first century one sign of hope for the future of Angola rested in the energy and inventiveness of its women. Luandan women had developed giant markets which kept the city fed and clothed. They bought their supplies through a global air-freight network which stretched west to Brazil and east to the Arabian Gulf. In the provinces women, supported by foreign-sponsored micro-credit, established a multiplicity of small-scale business enterprises which traded everything from clothes and vegetables to spare engine-parts for municipal buses. Female solidarity enabled women to support one another in times of crisis, even when jealous male politicians tried to interfere with their business plans by deploying a much-feared 'fiscal police' to harvest some of the profits. The robust nature of female enterprise in Angola crossed ethnic boundaries and was as dynamic among the Kongo of the north as among the Ovimbundu of the south.

The economic revival stretched throughout the country and was not only to be found in the burgeoning city of Luanda. In the south-west the plateau communities of white settlements had escaped the worst disruptions of war and old grassland traditions of cattle-keeping were adapted with modern methods of ranching and dairying. In the bursting city of Lubango the son of a Swiss mission family even opened a cheese factory. In the far north the revival of forest food crops for the market brought wealth back to the city of Uige at the heart of the former coffee groves. On the highland a stretch of the Benguela railway was restored to working order and Ovimbundu farmers were able to use it to supply fresh produce to the city Huambo. Angola began to look like a typical African country of westernised towns' men and women supported by market-oriented peasants. The country was administered by a highly-centralised, presidential, government, but it was a government that had been freely chosen in a popular election. Even the parliamentary opposition spoke optimistically about Angola's future prospects.

APPENDIX

THE CADBURY FACTOR IN ANGOLAN HISTORY

The firm of Cadbury Bros has rarely been out of the news. Until the 1960s it was a family business run largely by Quakers who had moved from making drinking cocoa to making iconic dairy milk chocolate bars. Thereafter it became a quoted stock exchange company booted like a football from owner to owner until by 2015 it was a part of Warren Buffet's global empire along with Heinz beans and Kraft processed cheese. The financial changes were always controversial: at one time the chairman was a former Tory minister for war, and when Kraft made its hostile bid there was a national outcry in Britain which reverberated through the media for years. But controversy was by no means new. Cadburys were prominently in the news a hundred years before the Kraft uproar. The issue was who should be patronised as the growers of the essential cocoa beans. Should it be Latin America, where chocolate had been the food of kings since the middle ages, or the Caribbean where Britain had plantations worked by freed slaves, or the Gold Coast where Protestant missionaries were seeking new sources of income for their converts, or should Cadbury Bros buy cocoa from the once coffee-growing islands of Portuguese West Africa?

The debate over cocoa supplies has generated a huge scholarly literature. Henry Nevinson talked about 'The Modern Slavery' of Portugal in Harper's magazine. By 1906 the Swiss missionary, Héli Chatelain, who had been campaigning against the slave trade for a decade, discreetly told his sponsors that the wide-scale sale of slaves from Angola to the cocoa islands was still in full flood, as reported by Nevinson. He said, moreover, that the most trustworthy witness to the slavery crisis was William Cadbury, in Birmingham, and his researcher on the ground, Joe Burtt. Chatelain was not discreet enough in his observations and in 1907 he was hounded out of Angola before the slavers could burn down his mission station. He was expelled on the trumped up charge that his wayside store, run on strictly teetotal lines, had failed to pay the local tax on rum, a commodity which other traders used to buy slaves. In 1908 Chatelain died in exile in Switzerland and Cadbury decided to visit Angola to see for himself how the family firm, over which he later came to preside, was sourcing its raw material. When Basil Davidson, the premier scholar-journalist of Africa, wrote a follow up to his 1954 analysis of 'slavery' in Angola he called his new book *Black Mother* and dedicated it to William Cadbury. Five years later a thesis on the earlier history of Angola was dedicated to Cadbury's daughter.

The flood of academic books on turn-of-the-century slavery in Angola began with James Duffy on *A Question of Slavery*. These books often concentrated on the controversy which erupted when William Cadbury published, initially for private circulation only, his book on *Labour in Portuguese West Africa*. The great campaigners against colonial injustice and exploitation did not always see eye to eye and the Cadburys were accused of hypocrisy and of being slow to stop buying slave-grown cocoa beans. Books such as Lowell Satre, *Chocolate on Trial* and Catherine Higgs, *Chocolate Islands: Cocoa, Slavery and Colonial Africa* dwelt extensively on the controversy. W.G. Clarence-Smith put the question of cocoa into a wider context in *Cocoa and Chocolate 1765–1914*. He pointed out that even when production passed from the white-owned slave plantations to black peasant farmers cocoa did not benefit African growers in the way that tea had enriched Japanese gardeners. Meanwhile in Angola slavery was replaced by a not dissimilar system of forced labour in which conscription was used to supply alternative, but less lucrative, sources of colonial wealth such as dried fish, corn meal, sugar cane and wild rubber.

The turning point in the Portuguese cocoa trade occurred, coincidentally or otherwise, around the time of William Cadbury's visit. It was a time of momentous change in Africa. Britain had recently conquered the Dutch mining republic of South Africa, Belgium decided to confiscate its king's private fiefdom in Congo, the French defeated some of the Muslim rulers of West Africa and Portuguese anarchists assassinated their king and his heir apparent. Relations between Portugal and its 'oldest ally', effectively its neo-colonial economic overlord, had not recovered from the ultimatum of 1890 when Lord Salisbury ordered Portugal to hand most of the Zambezi basin over to the diamond tycoon and political brigand Cecil Rhodes, who renamed the territories after himself, the Rhodesias. It was into this world that William Cadbury stepped—along with his young interpreter. The diary of his travels is very sparse, and his published report is tailored for public consumption. But he also wrote extensive letters home to his wife and they give a living picture of life in Portuguese Africa in 1908 and 1909.

Travel to Africa was on a 3000 ton Hull steamer carrying a Portuguese doctor and a vice-consul from São Tomé who both spoke some English and were kind to British travellers—including the sad telegraph operator being sent out to Moçâmedes in the deep desert of south Angola. Interesting Portuguese meals, each with a silver stand of tooth-picks, were the main subject of report, with biscuits and fruit at six in the morning, a breakfast of fish, omelettes and coffee at ten, followed four hours later by a lunch of sardines and cheese, afternoon tea, and then a full-blown dinner at six in the afternoon before the nine o'clock nightcap. The Birmingham industrialist missed having orange marmalade for breakfast but reassured the captain that he could make do with quince cheese, called *marmelo*, instead. Upper class passengers included a Portuguese Indian and his wife and several army officers. Subordinates travelled below deck and spent their time playing cards while those above indulged in chess, skittles and quoits. Many of the travellers were planters and Cadbury found them 'very pleasant' as he worked hard to learn Portuguese and comically shook hands with them before every meal. They compared their own estates with those Cadbury had visited in the West Indies. The cargo included a huge lighter on the front deck, a vessel to be used for ferrying cocoa sacks from shore to ship. The ship also carried three fine mules for plantation work, and several pet parrots. The rest of the livestock, oxen, sheep, ducks and rabbits were destined for the pot en route to the rocky Cape Verde island of St Vincent, a way station with its British coaling pier and the South American telegraph relay post staffed by eighty men.

On the island of Príncipe the rain had delayed the north-bound mail steamer from loading cocoa and so letters home could be sent. The times and dates of incoming and outgoing mail steamers were a constant source of concern. Portuguese passengers celebrated their arrival on the smaller of the two cocoa islands with a feast of dried cod, potatoes, garlic and cabbage, flooded with olive oil, followed by stewed rabbit. Cadbury was courteously welcomed by the managers of each of the great estates and travelled across the beautiful green island on a railway trolley pulled by mules. The planters explained that the great problem of Príncipe, in contrast to São Tomé, had been sleeping sickness which had decimated ill-fed Africans ever since the tsetse fly had been introduced on sailing vessels a hundred years before. Although labourers from Angola periodically brought the disease back again, the planters clothed them in cotton jerkins which were as sticky as fly-paper and claimed they had thus captured 200,000 flies. Although much feared, the flies were kept out of white plantation houses and one manager even had his white wife and baby daughter living on the estate, far removed from the half dozen other white women living in town. 'You can imagine the pluck needed', said Cadbury, 'to live and work against such odds and our kind hosts, and the doctor with whom we dined, were splendid examples of quiet, strong, men doing good work in an out of the way corner of the world'. In the town the English telegraph office had a very fine residence which served afternoon tea but refused to host the controversial visitors who were known to be investigating allegations of slavery. A savvy Lisbon merchant, by contrast, had sent instructions that Cadbury was to be given the apartment above his main store in the town and was to be generously dined, though not wined since he was a practicing Quaker, by the local manager, who was reported to be a 'capital fellow'. The visitors were supplied with Pears soap, tooth-paste, letter-paper, sealing wax, newspapers, cigars and mosquito nets. As dawn rose the little wooden town echoed with dogs, clocks and cockerels. On Sunday afternoon a white band master led his black musicians on to the town square for the entertainment of all those who had no conventional family life, having wisely left their wives at home in Europe. The band was so proficient that, in spite of being described as a mere 'nigger orchestra', it had won a prize at the Paris world fair.

When it came to business the kind but elderly acting governor of Príncipe cautiously referred all Cadbury's questions to the labour recruiting office. The peppery labour agent invited an important plantation owner to sit in on the Monday interview and then did his best to divert the conversation from its main topic, saying that in due course he would provide written information. The key question of repatriating migrant workers was one that some planters were willing to discuss but no government official would address. Cadbury was taken to an estate where women were sorting and drying cocoa beans in a manner that seemed to the visitor 'as much like play as work'! The estate hospital was said to be as clean as any in Europe. This may have been because it had recently been visited by the Portuguese crown prince who was being shown the glories of empire. But although the Englishmen travelled for miles through the plantations they never saw a field worker. The island had no schools, semi-ruined churches with seventeenth-century blue tiles, and very few priests. Old communities of semi-indigenous families had colonial traditions which preserved a self-perpetuating system of literacy. The 20-inch Decauville estate tramways were built by the French, using German iron, since the island had no English trading house. Peak Frean chocolate biscuits were on sale but most other consumer goods came from Germany.

By 1 November Cadbury and Burtt had reached the main island of São Tomé and were hosted by a Mr Levy. Jewish colonisation had begun on the island from the 1480s and four centuries later, when the persecution of Jews had abated to the point where Portugal even considered hosting a 'homeland' for Jews in Africa, Jewish entrepreneurs were important on all the Portuguese colonial islands and indeed on the mainland of Angola. Instead of a 'buggy', a heavy 'Victoria carriage', with four mules, hauled the guests up muddy tracks to an estate where workers were given a generous allowance of 3 pounds of cooked rice a day and 'allowed' to scavenge for fruit in the woods. Cadbury wanted to study the death rate, which was distressingly high, and the birth rate, which was extremely low, each of which reinforced the constant need for new recruits from the mainland. The next estate, although managed by 'a good-hearted master' who employed sixty-five white staff, was worked by 900 'help-less' black Angolans herded together in insanitary conditions with no latrines and limited washing facilities. Diseases spread readily after they had eaten 'unwholesome' scavenged food. The cold upland rain caused much suffering, though the log fires inside the smoky wooden barracks did keep the mosquitoes at bay. At 9 PM the plantation bell tolled for the flickering lights to be extinguished and then tolled again at 5 AM to summons everyone to roll call and send them off to work before the break of day. On one plantation the workers were allegedly given coffee with a dash of brandy before they began work. The meals were predominantly rice with some beans, dried fish and imported American beef. Cadbury thought that the island had few snakes and scorpions to endanger the bare-footed *serviçaes*. The most cheerful aspect of the estate consisted of a score or so of happy children, probably the illegitimate black off-spring of the white managers. The island had about 1,000 white foremen but none of the estates provided quarters for wives and the Edwardian indus-trialist did not dwell on alternative forms of quasi-marital partnerships.

Working life may have been long and harsh but when Cadbury was offered a fine horse to ride through the tropical vegetation below the 6000 foot mountains he became lyrical. His next visit was to a high and healthy model plantation whose manager had been given an earldom after hosting the crown prince. 40 square miles were worked by 2000 migrant workers who produced 50,000 bags of cocoa at a rate of 8 pounds of beans per prime ten-year-old tree. Some of the labourers had come from Mozambique and Cadbury deemed them to be 'cleaner and more civilised' than those from Angola, and he hoped they might help solve the critical shortage of labour on the island. Soon after he left this expectation was shattered when a major riot occurred among Mozambicans who had been told they had been hired on one-year contracts but were refused a passage home. Their wages were 12 shillings a month, but one third had been withheld to finance their return to Mozambique. Angolan workers, who had no expectation of ever returning home, earned less, up to 10 shillings for men and 6 for women. Pay day was the last Sunday of the month and on Sundays labourers on some estates only worked a half day and in the afternoon were paraded before visitors in clean cotton shifts. After the Sunday dinner the men engaged in wild dancing. The wages were, Cadbury supposed, the poorest agricultural pay in the whole world but he admired the supply of food, of clothing, and even the odd ounce of tobacco as a bonus. So enthusiastic was he that he suggested that one of his letters be shared with Rowntrees, another Quaker chocolate firm which bought Portuguese cocoa beans. He was particularly cheered that the men and women who operated the cocoa drying kilns sang while they worked but he did not mention that the temperature in the sheds could reach 110 degrees Fahrenheit.

For transport some short stretches of railway were steam-hauled and linked up to the 'charming' forest tracks used by mules. From the beaches surf boats manned by the communities of 'Angolares' who had been brought to the island 200 years before, carried cargo and passengers out to the coastal shipping. These old black settlers, 2000 or more of them, never worked on the cocoa estates but only on the 30-foot surf boats which they manned 'like Venetian gondoliers', their naked black backs glistening in the rain. In addition to the Angolares, São Tomé hired boatmen from Cabinda on the Congo mainland, and unlike the Angolans the boatmen had contracts which were honoured when the time came for them to go home. Two of them carried William Cadbury shoulder-high through the surf and paddled him out to the uncomfortable 180-ton cocoa launch which carried him to the next beach where he was warmly welcomed by a planter whom he had previously met on ship-board. A serious investigation of the slaving crisis felt almost like a semi-luxurious tropical holiday complete with romantic red sunsets and glorious moon-lit panoramas. Although some, if not most, planters were willing to discuss politics, when Cadbury got back to the island capital the 'friendly' governor was definitely not inclined to be helpful with the enquiry. And so he departed on the fifty-six hour voyage to Angola, arriving on 16 November 1908.

In Luanda harbour the steam ship *Cazengo* was about to sail north and so Cadbury was rowed out to her to see for himself the conscripted *serviçaes* it was carrying to São Tomé. He made no comment to his wife on their circumstances and wrote instead about his poor hotel bed and the 'niggers' who chattered all night in the street and prevented him from sleeping after his arduous row out to the ship in blistering sunshine. The American mission, which Chatelain had helped to establish twenty years before on behalf of the eccentric 'Bishop' Taylor, was now affiliated to the Methodist church and, taking pity on Cadbury, gave him a cool and airy room on the hill above the town. The mission administered a dozen inland stations and ran a city school where the children sang Methodist hymns from a Portuguese hymnal published in Chicago. The British coaling station put an office at Cadbury's disposal and supplied him with a backlog of newspapers. At government house the governor, Paiva Couceiro, was a young man recently recovered from a riding accident which had been so severe that no one had dared initially to tell him that the king and prince of Portugal had been assassinated. He apparently had an Irish mother and was deemed to be one of Angola's most dynamic military rulers. As in São Tomé, however, this governor was absolutely unwilling to give Cadbury any help, though he did permit him to travel around Angola and make his own enquiries. Meanwhile, colonial life carried on and Cadbury enthusiastically took part in a cricket match organised by a cable-laying vessel which called at Luanda, and challenged the chief engineer to a round of golf on the sand-spit of Luanda Island. Burtt also played tennis in the cool of the late afternoons. Life was expensive, however, and when entertaining the few British residents of Luanda at dinner in the hotel they were shocked to be charged three dollars for a Portuguese pudding made with sixty eggs. One of their guests was the British consul, H.G. Mackie, who was allegedly translating a history of the Angolan wars into English.

After a frustrating delay Cadbury took the Royal Trans-Africa Railway Company train inland from Luanda through stands of baobab trees, picnicking on board and noting the fifty 'boys' with filed teeth who had been recruited from the far north to complete the building of the railway as far as Malange. After a night stop at a rail-side inn they entered a tse-tse-infested forest where once thriving villages had been deserted owing to the recent pandemic of sleeping sickness. Cadbury remarked presciently that since the railway was losing £3000 to £4000 a year it was unlikely that capital would be raised to extend the line beyond Malange. His destination was the Monte Bello plantation, an estate reached by canopied hammock carried on springy palm ribs by two 'boys'. Cadbury was a very heavy man, however, and one of the porters sprained his ankle in a termite hole, so the passenger decided to walk up the path admiring the throngs of butterflies. Walking was something that Portuguese planters rarely did, though Héli Chatelain, who regularly traversed the district as a missionary in the 1880s, often walked to spare his porters. The estate had been built by the English import-export house of Newton and Carnegie, which had employed 300 slaves, but after the crash in coffee prices it had been sold for a pittance ten years before Cadbury's visit. The 200 workers still on the estate were allowed Sunday off to work their own vegetable plots. They were not people who had been 'hunted', in Cadbury's words, from the surrounding villages of free men and women, nor were they recruited from communities which supplied workers to the railway. Instead plantation labourers were 'bought' from much further afield at the cost of £18 a head. Cadbury said that they were, in his opinion, slaves but still he found the plantation beautiful with its stands of cinnamon, rubber, coffee, nutmeg, cocoa and sugar cane. The new owner received him with lavish Portuguese hospitality and when the day came to leave he put a whole roast suckling pig in the 'chop box' for a picnic on the train back to Luanda. As they left the owner set off for Cazengo, further up the line, to give evidence at the trial of men who had been remanded in gaol for three years after allegedly killing a white man. On their own downward journey they stopped for a wayside lunch with a German mining prospector whose English wife belonged to the Waddington family which was related to both Burtt and to Cadbury himself. She told them that it was eighteen months since she had spoken to another white woman, though Cadbury surmised that even she had been only half white. They quixotically discussed Quaker genealogies, and notably the Pumphrey sugar family, in this remote corner of Africa.

After returning to Luanda Cadbury headed south on a twenty-year-old coastal steamer built in Greenock to reach the great harbour of Lobito where Union Castle ships now called to reliably collect mail. Major Cunningham told him all about the new railway heading for the Transvaal, which now stretched 200 of its proposed 2000 kilometres into the interior. Already copper from the ancient Katanga mines was being brought to the railhead and Cunningham said he had paid his team of porters 300 oxen to carry his mineral trove. He shipped out 400 tons of copper and 200 of tin on a British cargo ship. A much-travelled Danish elephant hunter in Lobito claimed that he had been trading in local ivory for twenty years. Further south, at the desert harbour of Moçâmedes, Cadbury reported that 'in the town itself slavery pure and simple is the general order of things, especially for domestic service'. The town was employed curing dried fish for the São Tomé cocoa plantations. The death rate among conscripts from the highland was notoriously high and out in the sand a forlorn cemetery was surrounded by a mud wall to prevent jackals from digging up the corpses. The remote town hosted an important Atlantic cable station staffed by nine men and one woman from England. The Portuguese expatriates kept Cadbury awake at night because, since gambling was outlawed, they did not start playing cards in the hotel lounge until gone midnight and only finished at four in the morning, often surreptitiously accompanied by the chief of police who happened to be the brother of the governor. The travellers then headed back north on the steam ship *Malange* hoping to visit the notorious slaving harbour at Novo Redondo, at which they had been prevented from calling on their way south. Obstruction continued, however: with the ship anchored three miles off shore, Cadbury was advised that there was no hotel at which he could lodge in the town and no private household willing to receive him. In the end the recruiting agent agreed to meet him for breakfast and to answer any questions about labour migration. Embarrassment in the little town of kraals surrounded by fields of sugar cane turned out to have been caused when the agent arranged to ship a cargo of *serviçaes* to São Tomé on the *Malange*, little thinking that Cadbury would be returning north so soon. Cadbury was thus able to observe, and photograph, the loading of conscripted deck passengers.

To travel back south to Benguela Cadbury booked a passage on the proud 6000 ton *Lusitania*, currently on a trip to East Africa carrying passengers but not cargo. One of the passengers was a Portuguese baron who owned one of the biggest slave-buying agencies at Benguela. He bought slaves at between 12 and 16 pounds sterling and sold them on at not less than 20 pounds. Cadbury found it hard to be civil to this patronising man who smelt of scent and had recently been on holiday to Paris. On landing at Benguela the governor was alleged to be 'ill' and the labour agent had been instructed to shut down all business until the visitors left. The last shipment of slaves had been sent out on 10 October 1908 to ensure that it should arrive in São Tomé before Cadbury was expected there. When investigating the trail to the interior it was found to be still strewn with the bones of slaves who had died on their way down to the coast. For some traders and missionaries the railway facilitated the crossing of the barren coast and its escarpments but the great caravans still walked. Trekking inland for a few hours on the great trail to Bihé, Cadbury met 250 traders coming to the coast, mostly carrying rubber and beeswax, and was overtaken by 150 porters heading inland with bales of cotton textiles. The porters, many of whom might have been slaves, and some of whom were children, carried loads ranging from 20 to 80 pounds. The headman, wearing a hat and coat, carried nothing but everyone else was festooned with water calabashes, knives, guns, kegs of spirits, cooking pots, bags of meal and even a folding canvass chair for the boss. The white tourist caused great anxiety to the caravans and when Cadbury tried to photograph porters they sometimes fled in panic. The route was lined with funerary cairns, topped with little flags or rum bottles, remembering those who had died by the wayside. Some had been slaves in heavy wooden shackles which were discarded in the bush when they died or taken off to give the impression that they were 'free' when they reached the harbour. Cadbury picked up a few shackles but most of them had been gleaned by scavengers seeking scarce firewood which they could sell in a town surrounded by barren countryside. He would have liked to travel further into the 'veldt' to meet local villagers but he soon had to return to the stuffy, mosquito-ridden little harbour town. On Christmas day Cadbury boarded the *Ambaca* for one more week in Luanda and felt rather ungracious in refusing the three varieties of wine on the passengers' guest table but said that the bottles of imported Portuguese mineral water were excellent.

Luanda was described as a 'grand but somewhat mournful city' in which many of the fine old buildings on the main street were standing empty. It had no drainage system so that in hot weather the smell was dreadful; the street scavengers did not keep the streets clean, and at low tide the mud-flats around the bay were noxious. Burtt escaped from the heat and the smell by spending his last few days in Angola on a hunting trip south of Luanda Island, hoping to shoot a shy antelope at dawn or track a night-prowling leopard. Cadbury escaped the heat by spending his nights up the hill at the Methodist mission. One of the missionaries was writing the biography of an ex-slave who worked for him and which Cadbury hoped he would publish. Until then he had not realised what a risk the mission had taken by befriending him. The government was already suspicious of the mission's condemnation of the on-going trade in *serviçaes* but now the mission was really afraid that by receiving Cadbury as a guest it might have endangered all its works. Cadbury himself did not think that the Americans were at great personal risk but he felt bad to be leaving them with uncertainty hanging over them. He spent his last days in the hotel sorting out the mass of notes which he had collected for his report. He was able to get on with this 'tedious work' when a bank holiday was declared on the occasion of the governor's birthday, and he worked on when the cargo ship *Nigeria*, on which he was booked for the next leg north, was four days late. The British consul in Luanda, who had been dismayed that the Foreign Office in London had never publicised his own reports on the labour situation in Angola, much looked forward to the publication of Cadbury's assessment of the on-going traffic. Once on board a British ship Cadbury at last felt at ease with liberty, peace and comfort. He enjoyed the freedom, unknown in Portuguese high society, to walk about in his shirt sleeves and enjoy fresh butter and jam.

On the journey home the ship by-passed French Libreville but called at German Duala before reaching British Calabar. There Cadbury discovered among his correspondence why so many doors had been closed to him in Angola. A meeting at Caxton Hall in London on 4 December 1908 had obviously discussed the modern slave trade and had generated a new bitterness of feeling which he had not initially encountered among Portuguese hosts, whom he had always treated with frank openness and friendship. He now realised that when reports of the London meeting reached Luanda the director of the Angolan customs house had wanted to have him expelled from the country forthwith, much as Chatelain had been expelled two years earlier. On his way home Cadbury called for a couple of weeks at the Gold Coast and discussed the state of the peasant cocoa economy. Production there had the advantage that the coast had a dry season in which beans could be prepared for export without the need for the expensive drying kilns used on São Tomé. Hostile Portuguese accused Cadbury, the industrial spy, of wanting to patriotically shift his cocoa supply from Portuguese Africa to British Africa. As an alternative some critics even accused him of wanting to bankrupt the São Tomé plantation system so that British investors could buy up the cocoa land cheaply. Thus it was that Cadbury returned to Bourneville and stepped into the hornet's nest of controversy and litigation which generated the plethora of academic literature.

SELECT BIBLIOGRAPHY

Further reading in English

Margaret Anstee, *Orphan of the Cold War* (Macmillan, 1996).

R.T. Anstey, *Britain and the Congo in the Nineteenth Century* (Clarendon Press, 1962).

Gerald Bender, *Angola Under the Portuguese* (Heinemann, 1978).

David Birmingham, *Portugal and Africa* (Macmillan, 1999).

——, *Frontline Nationalism in Angola and Mozambique* (James Currey, 1992).

——, *A Concise History of Portugal* (Cambridge, 1993).

——, *Empire in Africa: Angola and its Neighbours* (Ohio, 2006).

David Birmingham and Phyllis M. Martin (eds), *History of Central Africa* (3 vols, Longman, 1993–98).

Charles Boxer, *Race Relations in the Portuguese Colonial Empire* (Oxford University Press, 1963).

William Boyd, *Brazzaville Beach* (Sinclair-Stevenson, 1990).

Inge Brinkman, *A War for People* (Köppe Verlag, 2005).

William Cadbury, *Labour in Portuguese West Africa* (Routledge, 1910).

Patrick Chabal *et al.*, *A History of Post-Colonial Lusophone Africa* (Hurst, 2002).

——, Patrick Chabal and Nuno Vidal (eds), *Angola: The Weight of History* (Hurst, 2007).

Chatham House, *Angola* (All-Party Parliamentary Reports for 2003 and 2006).

W.G. Clarence-Smith, *The Third Portuguese Empire* (Manchester, 1985).

——, *Slaves, Peasants and Capitalists in Southern Angola* (Cambridge, 1979).

Michael Comerford, *The Peaceful Face of Angola* (Privately published, Luanda, 2005).

Jacopo Corrado, *The Creole Elite and the Rise of Angolan Protonationalism, 1870–1920* (Cambria Press, 2008).

Basil Davidson, *The African Awakening* (Cape, 1955).

——, *Black Mother* (Victor Gollancz, 1961).

———, *In the Eye of the Storm: Angola's People* (Longman, 1972).

Jill Dias, 'Black Chiefs, White Traders and Colonial Policy' (*Journal of African History*, Cambridge, 1976).

———, 'Famine and Disease in the History of Angola' (*Journal of African History*, Cambridge, 1981).

James Duffy, *A Question of Slavery* (Oxford University Press, 1967).

Edward George, *The Cuban Intervention in Angola* (Cass in 2012).

F.A. Guimaraes, *The Origins of the Angolan Civil War* (Macmillan, 2001).

R.J. Hammond, *Portugal and Africa 1815–1910: A Study in Uneconomic Imperialism* (Stanford University Press, 1966).

Christine Hatzky, *Cubans in Angola* (University of Wisconsin Press, 2015).

Franz-Wilhelm Heimer (ed.), *Social Change in Angola* (Weltforum, 1973).

Beatrix Heintze (*et al.*, eds) *Angola on the Move* (Lembeck, 2008).

Linda Heywood, *Contested Power in Angola* (Rochester, 2000).

Catherine Higgs, *Chocolate Islands* (Ohio, 2012).

Tony Hodges, *Angola: from Afro-Stalinism to Petro-Diamond Capitalism* (James Currey, 2001).

Ryszard Kapuscinski, *Another Day of Life* (Picador, 1987).

S.E. Katzenellenbogen, *Railways and the Copper Mines of Katanga* (Clarendon Press, 1973).

Colin Legum and Tony Hodges, *After Angola* (Rex Collings, 1976).

Judith Listowel, *The Other Livingstone* (Friedman, 1974).

David Livingstone, *Missionary Travels in South Africa* (John Murray, 1857).

Karl Maier, *Angola: Promises and Lies* (Serif, 1996).

John Marcum, *The Angolan Revolution* (2 vols. M.I.T., 1969 and 1978).

João Pedro Marques, *The Sounds of Silence: Nineteenth Century Portugal and the Abolition of the Slave Trade* (Berghahn, 2006).

Pedro Mendes, *Bay of Tigers* (Granta, 2003).

Joseph Miller (*et al.*, eds), *A Scholar for All Seasons: Jill Dias 1944–2008* (*Portuguese Studies Review*, 2011) including a full catalogue of Jill Dias's thirty-four publications.

J.J. Monteiro, *Angola and the River Congo* (Macmillan, 1875).

Maria [São] Neto, 'In Town and Out of Town: A Social History of Huambo' (unpublished PhD dissertation, University of London, 2012).

Henry Nevinson, *A Modern Slavery* (Background Books, 1963).

Malyn Newitt, *Portugal in Africa* (Hurst, 1981).

Pepetela, *Mayombe* (Heinemann, 1983).

———, *Yaka* (Heinemann, 1996).

Michael Samuels, *Education in Angola 1878–1914* (Teachers College Press, 1970).

Lowell Satre, *Chocolate on Trial* (Ohio University Press, 2005).

J. Stockwell, *In Search of Enemies: A CIA Story* (André Deutsch, 1978).

Inge Tvedten, *Angola: The Struggle for Peace and Reconstruction* (Westview, 1997).

W.S. van der Waals, *Portugal's Wars in Angola* (Ashanti Publishing, 1993).

SELECT BIBLIOGRAPHY

John Frederick Walker, *A Certain Curve of Horn: the Hundred-Year Quest for the Giant Sable Antelope in Angola* (Grove Press, 2004).

Douglas Wheeler and René Pélissier, *Angola* (Pall Mall Press, 1971).

Michael Wolfers and Jane Bergerol, *Angola in the Front Line* (Zed Press, 1983).

Other Angolan Materials

Valentim Alexandre, *Velho Brasil Novas Áfricas: Portugal e o Império 1808–1975* (Afrontamento, 2000).

———, *Origens do Colonialism Português Moderno* (Sá da Costa, 1979).

Arlindo Barbeitos, *Portugal e Angola* (University of Beira, Ph.D., 2006).

A. Bastian, *Ein Besuch in San Salvador* (Bremen, 1859, Johnson Reprint 1970).

Drumond Jaime and Hélder Barber (eds), *Depoimentos para a história Recente* (privately published, Lisbon, 1999).

Marcelo Bittencourt, *Estamos Juntos: O MPLA e a luta anticolonial* (2 vols, Kilombelombe, Luanda, 2008).

Marina Rey Cabrera, *La Guerra de Angola* (Editora Politica, Havana, 1989).

H. Capello and R. Ivens, *De Benguela às Terras de Iacca* (Imprensa Nacional, Lisbon, 2 vols, 1881).

Cláudia Castelo, *O Modo Português de Estar no Mund: O Luso-Tropicalismo e a ideologia colonial portuguesa 1933–1961* (Afrontamento, 1998).

———, *Passagens para África: O Povoamento de Angola e Moçambique com Naturais da Metrópole 1920–1974* (Afrontamento, 2007).

Sócrates Dáskalos, *Um Testemunho para a História de Angola* (Vega, 2000).

Ralph Degado, *História de Angola* (4 vols, Magalhães, Lobito, 1955 and other editions).

———, *O Amor a 12 Graus de Latitude Sul* (Empresa Industrial Gráfica do Pôrto, 1935).

Jill Dias and Valentim Alexandre, *O Império Africano 1825–1890* (Editorial Estampa, 1998).

Carlos Estermannn, *Etnografia de Angola* (2 vols, IICT, Lisbon, 1983).

Aida Freudenthal, *Arimos e Fazendas* (Caxinde, Luanda, 2005).

Amavel Granger, *Facetas d'Angola* (Paris, 1926).

Henrique Guerra, *Angola: Estrutura Económica e Classes Sociais* (Edições 70, 1979).

Philip Havik (*et al.*, eds), *Caminhos Cruzados em História e Antropologia: Ensaios de Homenagem a Jill Dias* (Imprensa de Ciências Sociais, 2010).

Beatrix Heintze, *Pioneiros Africanos* (Caminho, 2004).

———, *A África Centro-Ocidental no Século XIX* (Kilombelome, Luanda, 2014).

———, *Ethnographische Aneignungen: Deutsche Forschungsreisende in Angola* (Lembeck, 1999).

Lawrence Henderson, *A Igreja em Angola* (Além-Mar, 1990).

Isabel Castro Henriques, *Percursos da Modenidade em Angola* (IICT, Lisbon, 1997).

António de Assis Júnior, *Relato dos Acontecimentos de Dala Tando e Lucala* (Edições 70, 1980).

——, *O Segredo da Morta* (Edições 70, 1979).

Lúcio Lara, *Um Amplo Movimento* (3 vols, 1996–2006, privately published).

——, *Imagens de um percurso* (Luanda, 2009).

Júlio de Castro Lopo, *Paiva Couceiro* (A.G.U, Lisbon, 1968).

Ladislaus Magyar, *Reisen in Süd-Afrika* (Pest, 1859).

João Pedro Marques, *Portugal e a escravatura dos africanos* (Imprensa de Ciências Sociais, 2004).

——, *Sá da Bandeira e o fim da escravidão* (Imprensa de Ciências Sociais, 2008).

Norton de Matos, *Memórias e Trabalhos da Minha Vida* (Editora Marítimo-Colonial, 4 vols, 1944–45).

Christine Messiant, *L'Angola colonial, histoire et société* (Schlettwein, 2006).

Carlos Pacheco, *MPLA: um nascimento polémico* (Vega, 1997).

Didier Péclard, *Les incertitudes de la nation en Angola: aux racines sociales de l'Unita* (Karthala, 2015).

——, *Ethos Missionnaire et Esprit du Capitalisme: La Mission Philafricaine en Angola* (Lausanne University, M.A. 1993).

René Pélissier, *Les Guerres Grises* (Montamets, 1977).

——, *La Colonie du Minautaure* (Montaments, 1978).

——, *Explorar: Voyages en Angola et autres Lieux Incertains* (Montamets, 1979) all privately published.

Pepetela, *A Geração da Utopia* (Dom Quixote, 1992).

——, *Predadores* (Dom Quixote, 2005).

——, *Jaime Bunda, Agente Secreto* (Dom Quixote, 2001).

F. Latour da Veiga Pinto, *Le Portugal et le Congo au XIXe Siècle* (Presses Universitaires de France, 1972).

Serpa Pinto, *Como eu Atravessei África* (2 vols, Samson Low, London, 1881).

José de Almeida Santos, *A Alma de uma Cidade* (Luanda City Council, 1973) and four other vols.

Maria Emilia Madeira Santos (ed.), *Viagens e Apontamentos de um Portuense em África: Diário de António Ferreira da Silva Porto* (Coimbra, 1986).

Maria da Silva, *Cadernos de Jill Dias: Inventário de um Arquivo* (CRIA, 2011).

Castro Soromenho, *Terra Morta* (Sá da Costa, 1949).

Jean-Michel Mabeko Tali, *O MPLA perante si próprio 1962–1977* (2 vols, Nzila, Luanda, 2001).

Georg Tams, *Visita as Possessões Portugezas na Costa Occidental d' Africa* (2 vols, Tipographia da Revista, Porto, 1850).

Ana Paula Tavares and Catarina Madeira Santos, *Africae Monumenta: A Apropriação da Escrita pelos Africanos* (IICT, Lisbon, 2002).

Rolf Peter Tschapek, *Bausteine eines zukünftigen deutschen Mittelafrika* (Steiner Verlag, 2000).

INDEX